D0001491

The White-Tailed Deer

NUMBER TWENTY-FIVE:
The Louise Lindsey Merrick
Natural Environment Series

The White-Tailed Deer

By

Ilo Hiller

Texas A&M University Press
College Station

Copyright © 1996 by Ilo Hiller
Manufactured in the United States of America
All rights reserved
First edition

The paper used in this book meets the minimum requirements
of the American National Standard for Permanence
of Paper for Printed Library Materials, Z39.48-1984.
Binding materials have been chosen for durability.

Library of Congress Cataloging-in-Publication Data

Hiller, Ilo, 1938–
     The white-tailed deer / by Ilo Hiller. — 1st ed.
          p.   cm. — (The Louise Lindsey Merrick natural
     environment series ; no. 25)
     Includes bibliographical references (p.   ) and
     index.
     ISBN 0-89096-697-4
     1. White-tailed deer.   I. Title.   II. Series.
QL737.U55H54   1996
599.73'57—dc20   95-47480
                                            CIP

Contents

Illustrations

Introduction

The white-tailed deer is a graceful, shy, and secretive animal that learns to hide and be elusive from the time it is born until it dies. Just catching sight of a wild deer bounding across the countryside or leaping a fence can be a thrilling experience for young and old alike. Knowing where and when to look makes watching this magnificent member of the deer family a year-round adventure.

Rural areas where there are open fields and nearby woodlands or other cover are the most promising areas to find deer, and a car parked beside a country road makes a good "blind" to sit in while waiting for the deer to show themselves. The first and last hours of daylight are usually the best viewing times since deer come out to feed in the open fields and meadows at those times of the day. They continue to feed and rest in these open areas at night while darkness serves as cover. During the day they seldom venture too far from some type of protective cover and are more likely to stay hidden from view, bedding down in heavier vegetation or woodlands. Tracks will confirm that they are in an

Landowners may use artificial feeders to attract deer and other wildlife; however, when range conditions are poor, too much supplemental feeding can compound an overpopulation problem and postpone nature's culling

area, but deer are masters at hiding. A buck standing motionless behind a bush or in a grove of trees or brush blends into his surroundings. He looks like part of the scenery, and he can be gone in the blink of an eye.

Many states have published wildlife viewing guides to help people locate areas where deer and other wildlife can be seen. These guides have been developed through national "watchable wildlife" programs, and each site described in the guides has been selected by a panel of wildlife professionals and other people knowledgeable about the area. State wildlife agencies should be contacted for information about their watchable wildlife programs and viewing guides.

Most landowners know where the deer on their property can be found. Some even set up artificial feeders near their homes to attract deer, and they enjoy watching the animals gather every evening to feed. Talking with local people in a rural town café over a cup of coffee may result in an invitation to view deer on private property. Permission must always be obtained from the owner before entering any private property to look for deer.

State and national parks, preserves, and refuges are also good places to see deer, and the rangers working there usually know where the best viewing sites are located. Large numbers of deer are commonly found on these lands, and the animals tend to become more tolerant of the presence of people. Deer may walk through the campsites, especially at night, and they often bed down nearby. At times, these "park" deer may appear to be almost tame, but they are still wild animals and their actions can be unpredictable. Visitors may be tempted to use picnic food to coax the deer closer, but this practice is discouraged because the food can upset the animal's digestive system and it may lead to a dangerous encounter between the deer and the park visitor. Binoculars can provide fine viewing and still allow the visitor to remain at a safe distance.

This book provides an in-depth look at the white-tailed deer, including information about habitat needs, food preferences, physical characteristics, antler development, social behavior, and general life cycle. Efforts have been made to include information that applies to whitetails throughout their range; if there is a southern bias here, it reflects both the large white-tailed deer populations in these states and the fact that the author spent thirty years with the Texas Parks and Wildlife Department.

The White-Tailed Deer

Related Animals and Deer Distribution

White-tailed deer belong to the family *Cervidae,* which contains as many as forty different species of large, hoofed mammals. This family is divided into four main categories: deer, moose, elk, and caribou, which are also known as reindeer. Although members of the family are spread throughout most of the world, they are considered native to the Americas, Europe, and Asia. They can be found from the mountains to the sea, living in or around the edges of tropical jungles, dense forests, brushlands, grassy plains, prairies, mountain meadows, marshes, swamps, and even the harsh Arctic tundra.

There is a wide range of sizes within the family. The largest is the North American moose, standing six to seven feet tall at the shoulders and weighing about fifteen hundred pounds; Alaska moose eight feet tall, weighing more than a ton, also have been recorded. The smallest member of the family is the South American pudu. This little deer stands about one foot tall at the shoulders and weighs less than twenty pounds.

Although all the species within the family are different, they have many things in common. They are all plant eaters, and they digest their food in a four-part stomach. They have long, thin legs with powerful muscles designed for running and jumping. They walk on two middle toes that have evolved into tough divided hooves. They have large round eyes to help them see approaching danger, and big ears that turn to catch sounds from all directions. They have long slender necks, and they are the only animals that can grow antlers, although not all of them do.

The male deer is called a buck, the female is a doe, and the young are fawns. Cattle terms are used to describe the sexes for moose, elk, and caribou: males are bulls, the females are cows, and the young are calves.

Deer species can be found in many parts of the world, but white-tailed deer and mule deer live primarily in the Western Hemisphere. It is believed that their ancestors may have crossed over from Asia some fifteen million years ago on an isthmus between Siberia and Alaska, becoming separated from others of their kind. This allowed these two species to evolve in the relative isolation of the American continents.

When mountains, large rivers, or other such physical barriers isolate animals for a long period and prevent them from getting together with other populations of their kind, subspecies may evolve. Although subspecies of the same species can interbreed and produce fertile offspring, lack of contact between them usually keeps this from happening. However, during the passage of time, the ranges of two subspecies occasionally overlap, allowing them to mix and blend into one. Researchers currently recognize at least thirty-eight white-tailed deer and eleven mule deer subspecies.

Whitetails are found from southern Canada to the South American countries of Venezuela and Colombia, but they seldom inhabit the high mountain regions of their range. Since warm-blooded animals from colder climates tend to be larger in size than their relatives in more temperate environments, it is not surprising that white-tailed deer living in the northern United States and Canada are larger than those found in the southern United States, Mexico, and Central and South America.

The northern woodland deer is the largest of the whitetail subspecies. It also has the widest range, stretching from Nova Scotia to southern Maryland in the east and across the continent north of the Ohio River to a western boundary at the Mississippi River. A mature northern woodland whitetail buck can weigh more than two hundred pounds. A mature nonpregnant doe usually weighs 60 to 75 percent of the buck's weight.

Florida's key deer is the smallest of the whitetails. A mature buck can weigh up to eighty pounds, but the doe seldom exceeds sixty-five pounds. This deer lives on the islands south of Miami from Little Pine Key to Sugar Loaf Key. It is an endangered species, its population estimated to be only about six hundred animals. Human use of its habitat for residential and commercial purposes is a major threat, and pet dogs create other problems for this small deer. Many people consider the key deer a nuisance because it feeds on cultivated and ornamental plants, but others view this distinctive, diminutive deer as a tourist attraction.

Whitetails are usually popular animals, and have been named the state mammal for Illinois, Mississippi, New Hampshire, Pennsylvania, and South Carolina. Although as many as twenty-six million whitetails may live in the contiguous forty-eight states, they are rarely found in Nevada, California, or Utah. The majority are located in the eastern, midwestern, and southern states, and more than three million of them are distributed throughout Texas. With the exception of the isolated Carmen Mountain whitetail *(Odocoileus virginianus carminus)* in the Big Bend National Park area of the state, Texas white-tailed deer are usually classified under one subspecies, *O.v. texanus.* A half-century of statewide trapping, releasing, and restocking efforts combined with expanding and overlapping deer ranges have contributed to a blending of the three other whitetail subspecies originally found within the state. When the last remaining area with suitable habitat but few or no deer was stocked in January, 1994, the state wildlife agency brought to a successful conclusion the task of restoring the whitetail, a deer that had been shot out on most of its ranges in the early 1900s.

Two mule deer subspecies dominate the Pacific Coast from California to Alaska. The Columbian black-tailed deer prefers the southern part of this range and the Sika black-tailed deer roams the northern part. Mule deer are found mostly in the western states, and they can live throughout the plains areas where buttes, draws, and stream bottoms provide suitable habitat. In Texas, desert mule deer roam the Trans Pecos region and the Rocky Mountain mule deer occurs in the canyon lands of the Panhandle.

When the ranges of mule deer and white-tailed deer overlap, their choice of habitat often segregates them during the breeding season. For example, in the northeastern foothills of the Rocky Mountains, mule deer prefer the hilly uplands while whitetails roam the narrow, wooded river bottoms of that area. During the winter they share the lower slopes. Distribution of the two species is reversed in Arizona with whitetails on the higher slopes and desert mule deer on the lower slopes and desert floor. In the Big Bend region of Texas, whitetails also prefer the higher elevations while the desert mule deer roam the intervening deserts.

However, the two may also share the lower elevations at times.

Changes in traditional mule deer habitat, such as invading brush and agricultural development, are allowing the whitetail slowly to expand its range westward into mule deer territory. As a result, white-tailed deer are increasing in the West while mule deer numbers have declined in many traditional ranges. During the 1960s mule deer in Montana outnumbered white-tailed deer by at least two to one. Today the whitetail population almost equals that of the mule deer.

Breeding between mule deer and white-tailed deer is possible, and deer with characteristics of both species have been reported. Biologists believe that the successful courtship probably involved a persistent whitetail buck and a mule deer doe. Since whitetail does are usually too elusive to be bred easily by a mule deer buck, it is more likely that mule deer are having more mixed fawns than are whitetails.

White-tailed deer have been introduced into several foreign countries, and the success of these transplants has been varied. The deer did poorly in the British Isles, but they met with more success in Czechoslovakia, Yugoslavia, Finland, and New Zealand. Brief accounts of a few of these transplants were published by the Wildlife Management Institute in *White-Tailed Deer Ecology and Management*. These accounts show that in some cases the deer introductions have been too successful, resulting in overpopulation.

Czechoslovakia imported thirty-one deer from 1890 to 1906. The animals quickly adapted to the country and their reproduction rate allowed small annual harvests to begin in 1911. From 1928 through 1935, hunters removed twelve to thirty deer each year. By 1936, the deer population had increased to 240 animals and more of them could be harvested. Hunting pressure is allowed to keep the deer population between 100 and 150 animals.

Twelve does and nine bucks were sent to Yugoslavia between 1970 and 1973. Although a few died during shipment, the remaining animals managed to reproduce at a steady rate and regular hunting began in 1980. These deer are located northwest of Belgrade in the forested areas along 124 miles of the Danube River. By 1983, the deer population had grown to four hundred animals.

The free ranging white-tailed deer population in Finland was started from five fawns—one buck and four does—which arrived in Helsinki in September, 1934. This shipment of deer was sponsored by Finnish emigrants in America who wanted to "enrich the wildlife of the forests of Finland by sending over the sea the most beautiful and noblest animal of our new home areas." By 1950 there were two hundred whitetails in Finland, and the next ten years saw the population increase to at least a thousand deer. Although severe winter weather can remove as much as 7 percent of the herd, the whitetails have always managed to recover.

Deer hunting was allowed in Finland for the first time in 1958, but only does could be harvested. The first bucks were not hunted until 1961. The population continued to grow, and special licenses had to be issued for shooting nuisance deer in fields and gardens. In an effort to control the deer population and prevent agricultural damage caused by deer, new hunting regulations were introduced allowing each hunter to kill either one doe or three fawns. Updated information from Kaarlo Nygren at the Finnish Game and Fisheries Research Institute indicates that the deer population reached its peak in the early 1990s when wintering whitetails numbered between twenty-two and twenty-three thousand animals. By 1993 the population had been reduced to eleven thousand deer, partially due to a dramatic increase of lynx and other deer predators. The recent winter population is estimated to be between twelve and thirteen thousand deer.

White-tailed deer in New Zealand were imported to South

Island and Stewart Island. The North American deer quickly adapted to the reversed seasons of the Southern Hemisphere. Antler rubbing in New Zealand starts in February, and by March all of the bucks have fully hardened and polished antlers. Rutting starts in mid-April, peaks during May, and the antlers are cast in October and November. Fawns are usually born from mid-December through January, and multiple births are rare.

Nine deer were released in 1905 at the head of Lake Wakatipu on the South Island of New Zealand. This is an area of glacial valleys with steep slopes, and the higher elevations have permanent snow fields and glaciers. Heavy snowfalls are common, with the average temperature ranging from 86 to 14 degrees Fahrenheit. Less than 850 deer live in the river valleys and the lower altitudes of the northeasterly slopes. They have been in poor physical condition for a number of years, and fawn survival is low. Farmers in the region limit hunter access to protect this small population of deer.

Also in 1905, two bucks and seven does were released on Stewart Island. This smallest and most southerly of the main islands of New Zealand is mountainous, except for the swamplands of the Freshwater River valley, and temperatures range from 81 to 30 degrees Fahrenheit with no extremes of heat and cold. By 1926, the growing whitetail population was having an impact on the island's vegetation, so the government placed a bounty of twenty cents on each deer tail. The bounty, being so small, did not encourage many people to help reduce the deer population. Between 1937 and 1952, teams of professional government hunters managed to kill 6,380 deer, about 30 percent of them whitetails and the rest red deer. Selective poisoned bait experiments conducted in 1980 proved that 75 percent of the deer on a test area could be removed by this method. Opposition from hunters and the general public probably would prevent poisoning from being used to thin the herd today. Sportsmen can remove about a thousand whitetails each year, but this number is still too small to counteract the animals' negative impact on the vegetation of the island.

In times past, animal introductions often were made with little or no thought given to the negative side of the picture. If environmental impact studies had been required, some of these foreign introductions of whitetails might not have occurred. Releasing axis, sika, and fallow deer into native white-tailed deer habitat in Central and South Texas during the 1950s might also have been avoided. These "exotic" deer were not subject to the limited hunting season established for native whitetails, so many Texas landowners imported them to provide year-round hunting opportunities on private game ranches. All went well until the exotic deer increased and many of them, escaping from these private ranches, began to have an impact on whitetails in the area. Food studies showed that axis and sika deer had the same food preferences as whitetails and were in direct competition with them. On ranges where nutritious, leafy plants favored by whitetails were severely depleted, the exotics merely shifted their diet to grass and thrived. Whitetails faced malnutrition and starvation because they could not sustain themselves on a diet of grass.

Competition and survival studies comparing sika and axis deer species with whitetails were conducted during the 1970s on three 96-acre, deer-proof pastures on the Kerr Wildlife Management Area in Texas. Three years prior to the study, all grazing animals were removed from these pastures to allow preferred deer foods to grow. Two sika bucks, four sika does, and a similar herd of whitetails were trapped and placed in one of the 96-acre pastures in January, 1971. Six axis bucks, four axis does, and a similar herd of whitetails were placed in a second pasture at the same time. The third pasture received only whitetails, two bucks and four does. No hunting was allowed on any of the pastures, and the animals were left to increase and compete for the available food without interference.

By April, 1974, there were fifteen whitetails and sixteen sika deer in the sika-whitetail pasture. During a drought in the summer of 1975, competition for food became severe. The shortage of nutritious food reduced the whitetail herd to six deer, but the sika herd increased to thirty-two during the same period. There were sixty-two sika deer and only three whitetails in the pasture by December, 1979, and these remaining three whitetails died in February, 1980.

In the axis-whitetail pasture, there were nineteen axis and eleven whitetails by December, 1975. A winter die-off in 1979 reduced the axis herd to fifteen and the whitetails to six. Only three nonbreeding whitetails remained at the end of 1979.

Whitetails in the third control pasture established a relatively stable population with a high of seventeen deer in 1974, a low of eleven deer during the drought of 1975, and a total of fourteen deer remaining in December, 1979. This long-term study illustrates the impact imported animals can have on native species and the habitat.

Despite competition with other species, changing land uses, habitat losses, and human encroachment, whitetails continue to prosper, and in many portions of their range, an increasing deer population is the primary problem facing agencies that manage this wildlife resource. Although the whitetail population in the contiguous United States is usually estimated to be about fourteen million deer, data presented at the Third International Congress on the Biology of Deer, held in Edinburgh, Scotland, in 1994, placed this estimated population closer to twenty-six million. This much higher number, based on 1993–94 estimated population figures provided by the individual states, surpasses the estimated worldwide population of twenty-five million.

Habitat and Food

As their wide distribution indicates, white-tailed deer can meet their needs in almost every ecological type, but they are most often associated with brushlands and forested areas. Pine and oak woodlands, dense stands of cottonwoods, mesquite bottomlands, and even tropical forests provide suitable habitat; however, a deer cannot live long in a mature forest where dense shade does not allow ground plants to survive. When logging practices remove some of the trees and allow the understory vegetation to grow again, deer numbers increase. Open areas and fields become excellent feeding sites because shrubs, tender grass shoots, and other suitable ground plants can grow there. Thicker vegetation and wooded areas nearby provide cover in which the deer can take shelter or escape from predators.

Marshes, canyons, brushlands, prairies, pasture lands, and meadows and fields are a few of the other places white-tailed deer can be found. Although shrubby or woody vegetation is not an absolute necessity, deer living in open grasslands usually have some type of screening or protective cover that can be used for

Deer often feed in open areas edged by trees and brush that provide shelter and escape routes. Removing woodland trees to create open spaces or corridors increases the amount of edge habitat and provides a wider diversity of food, shelter, and habitat components for deer. Courtesy Texas Parks and Wildlife Department.

escape purposes. Historically, deer in the Great Plains were found primarily along the major streams and their tributaries. As woody vegetation spread into the prairies and plains, deer were able to extend their ranges as well. Grazing lands comprised of prairies, plains, and forests are the primary habitat for deer in the western United States.

Deer prefer areas where two vegetative types such as woods and fields or grasslands and brush come together. This edge effect provides a wider diversity of food, shelter, and habitat components. Woodlands become more suitable for deer when trees are removed from small areas or corridors to increase the amount of edge habitat available. A creek or waterway running through a mixed-growth forest with open areas or corridors for feeding and movement could be described as ideal deer habitat in many parts of their range. It could provide food, water, shelter, and escape routes with little or no exposure to danger. Deer are strong swimmers, and they do not hesitate to cross large streams within their home ranges. They may use water to escape from a predator, or they may partially submerge themselves in it to escape biting flies and mosquitoes.

Although whitetails can subsist for long periods on water obtained from vegetation, available drinking water is a significant component in their habitat. Its importance to deer is emphasized by the fact that watering sites are frequently the centers of their home ranges, especially in desert or arid habitat. The presence or absence of water can noticeably affect their daily activities. A greater need for water in summer means that deer must remain near water or travel some distance between feeding and watering sites. Because traveling requires energy, more food is needed to make up for this expenditure of energy. As a result, when water is scarce, deer tend to concentrate wherever it is available rather than travel considerable distances on a daily basis.

Deer will drink from any water source, especially ditches or temporary puddles that form after a rain. Because an established watering hole can be a dangerous place where predators might lie in wait, most deer approach with extreme caution, drink quickly, and then leave. They almost never stop to eat while approaching the drinking site. They appear to be quite nervous, raising their heads frequently to look about as they drink. They may check their surroundings a couple of times each minute and usually spend no more than five minutes at the watering site. Does with fawns are the most cautious when approaching the water, and a single deer is more cautious than a group of bucks or does. If other wild animals are present, a deer may leave immediately or it may circle the area two or three times and then leave without approaching the water. When cattle are present, a deer may stare at them, stomp its front feet, walk back and forth, circle the area, and still leave without drinking.

The amount of water deer need varies with the time of year, weather, food, and the level of activity. They may consume as little as a quart or as much as five quarts a day. In the spring when new plant growth contains a lot of moisture, or when heavy rains add moisture to the vegetation, deer do not need to drink as much. They also lick the heavy morning dew from leaves when humidity is high. The most drinking water is usually needed in the summer when temperatures are higher and the water content of plants is low. Consequently, from May through September, most deer drink twice a day. Does in advanced stages of pregnancy and does with fawns may come to drink more often because the does need more water for the production of milk. In winter deer usually drink only once a day, and snow can meet their needs for moisture in areas where surface water is frozen.

Most of the people who study whitetails agree that sunset to dark is the period of greatest drinking activity for deer, but their findings may differ regarding other drinking periods throughout the year. Studies in Arizona indicate that daylight–sunrise and sunset–dark were the two drinking periods for whitetails in that state, with the heaviest daily use of water holes from shortly after sunset until midnight. Studies of whitetails in South Texas during the summer have shown that 7:00 A.M. and 11:00 A.M. are peak drinking periods in the morning. The evening peak period may last from 4:00 to 6:00 P.M., but visits to watering sites by some deer may occur at any time during the night.

Other information gained during a South Texas study showed

Water demands vary with the time of year, weather, food, and activity level. Deer may drink only once a day in winter, and snow can meet moisture needs when surface water is frozen. Courtesy Texas Parks and Wildlife Department.

that deer had a tendency to drink longer on their daily visit to water during the winter than they did during their more frequent visits in summer. They also drank longer during the warmer stages of the day than during the cooler portions in all months and at all seasons. There did not seem to be a set relationship between drinking and feeding. Some deer drank just before feeding, some just after, and for some there appeared to be no correlation between drinking and food gathering.

White-tailed deer are considered resident animals with fairly restricted home ranges. If they have food, water, and vegetation that will hide and shelter them, most deer spend an entire lifetime in an area no larger than a few hundred acres. At any given time a deer will be living on 200 to 350 acres. As time passes, its home range may shift within the same basic area to a slightly different 200 to 350 acres. During its lifetime, a deer's range may have included no more than a thousand acres. Movement studies in Texas have shown that whitetails usually stay within a mile and a half to three miles of their birthplace. Young fawns have small ranges, but expand these to match those of their mothers as they grow older. When a young buck is old enough to leave his family group, he must establish his own range or adopt the home range of whatever group he joins. These pioneering young bucks provide gene flow and may reestablish deer numbers in areas where habitats have improved enough to sustain them. An adult buck's home range is usually larger than a doe's. Although he may leave his home range during the breeding season while trailing a doe, he eventually returns. A deer chased by dogs may run several miles outside its range, but it generally circles around and ends up close to home again.

Movement within the home range is determined by seasonal food supplies, the need for cover or protection, and breeding requirements. In northern or mountainous areas where there are extreme seasonal differences in weather, whitetails usually have summer and winter ranges. Although whitetails are not migratory in the true sense of the word, they do move in winter from higher to lower elevations or into protected areas where browse plants are still available and the snow is less deep. In winter, deer in western areas head for protected valleys and the riparian zones, which are corridors of vegetation along the rivers and streams. Southern deer occupy the same ranges all year long. Home ranges are often larger in northern climates, and deer living in more open habitats may have larger home ranges than deer living in areas with heavy vegetation.

Although the sizes of deer ranges vary, all home ranges have two things in common. The range must be large enough to meet the deer's needs, but small enough for the deer to become familiar with every bush and tree in it. A deer's survival often depends upon a thorough knowledge of its habitat by sight, sound, and smell. Their commitment to home ranges is illustrated by the fact that during times of nutritional stress, deer have been known to starve to death on a barren home range—apparently unaware of possible food sources quite nearby—rather than leave. When deer are aware of a more distant food source, they will leave their normal home ranges to meet their needs.

Studies of penned deer in Pennsylvania indicate that a deer weighing 100 to 150 pounds needs four to six pounds (6,300 to 9,900 calories) of high-quality food daily to meet its needs. Smaller deer, weighing fifty to sixty pounds, can get by on as little as two pounds (3,600 calories). In the wild, the amount of food required may be greater, especially when range conditions are poor and the calorie content is reduced.

White-tailed deer do not stand in one spot and graze on vegetation, as a cow or horse does. Instead, these very selective feeders take a bite here, a nibble there, and then move on. They sniff and choose each leaf or plant part to be eaten, as if they know which ones are beneficial. Because the most nutritious plant tissues, called meristems, are found at the tips of most vegetation, the tip-feeding deer are usually eating this high-quality new growth. They pass over the less desirable forage as long as other food is available. Only when a deer is near starvation will it stuff its belly with coarse, stringy grass or other vegetation that has little or no nutritional value.

The animal's wide distribution and the habitat differences across this vast range make it difficult to characterize the whitetail's diet other than by the categories of browse, forbs, grasses, fruits, and nuts (mast). Flexibility in the diet helps a deer adapt to the vegetation changes that take place in its home range all year long. Whitetails can get nourishment from at least six hundred different plant species, but any individual can eat only those plants that grow in its own feeding areas during each season of the year. When other food is available, they eat very little grass, except for the tender and green new growth. They browse on tender leaves and the young shoots of woody plants and vines; however, they prefer to eat weeds and other broadleaf flowering plants, which are called forbs. If sheep and goats are present on the same range, they compete with deer for the available forbs and browse.

Browse is the primary food for whitetails in colder climates, and during the fall and winter seasons it makes up 60 to 80 percent of their diet in northwestern and north-central habitats. This browse is supplemented by whatever mast, forbs, and grasses are available at the time. Hollies, greenbriar, juniper, and other woody plants that do not shed their leaves are heavily used in winter ranges in the South and West. Forbs are the preferred food items for deer in the Coastal Bend area of Texas, which has a growing season close to three hundred days. Browse takes second place on the menu, and cool-season grasses make up another 15 percent in mid- to late winter. In the more arid South Texas habitats, browse and mast are the mainstays for deer, but forbs are preferred when available.

In some areas of the country during autumn, whitetails rely heavily on waste grain left behind by the harvesting process. They can thrive in close association with humans, benefiting from agricultural practices. Unfortunately, the deer's feeding habits do not make it a welcome visitor before the crops are harvested. Clashes with people result when deer visit fields and orchards to eat corn, wheat, other grains, legumes, vegetables, or fruits. Apples are an all-time favorite, and a deer can catch the scent of this delicious fruit from half a mile away. Except for shooting, about the only way to keep deer out of gardens and orchards is to erect a deer-proof fence. A height of at least ten to twelve feet is recommended because hungry deer easily jump an eight-foot fence.

Deer also browse on ornamental trees, shrubs, plants, and flowers growing around homes, a feeding activity that is not well received by homeowners. Scare tactics, such as noise or fluttering objects, will not stop deer for long. They quickly learn that the noise is harmless, and hunger can overcome the fear of anything except a direct threat. One way to lessen the problem is to plant things that deer do not particularly like to eat. Tough, hardy, aromatic plants which contain unpalatable terpines, tannin, and essential oils are usually rejected by deer. Many plants that produce a strong odor when the leaves are crushed fall into this category, but deer do not pass them by just because of the smell. They avoid them because they have learned that these plants interrupt their digestive processes. The chemicals in these plants bind with the proteins in the deer's food, making them indigestible. Sage, ceniza, most kinds of junipers, primrose jasmine, butterfly bush, wax myrtle, aloe, English ivy, and cherry and mountain laurels are some of the plants they seldom eat. A local horticulturist should be able to make additional suggestions about deer-resistant plants; however, a deer faced with starvation will eat almost anything. Repellents, both natural and commercial, can be used, but their effectiveness lasts only until the smell is gone or until they are washed into the soil. Commercial repellents contain such ingredients as bone tar oil, hot pepper sauce, fermented egg solids, and ammonium soaps. Keeping deer away from home gardens and plantings usually requires more effort and expense than it is worth.

When lakes and ponds are present in their home range, whitetails may visit these sites daily in the summer to feed on the floating vegetation. Does tend to munch on the aquatic plants in water no deeper than their bellies, but bucks have been observed feeding with only their necks and heads above the water.

Nuts, wild fruits and berries, lichens, mushrooms, and other fungi are added to the menu when they are in season. If mesquite beans are available, deer feed on them into midwinter. Finding a good supply of acorns allows a deer to put on its winter fat in a few days, building up a reservoir of energy that is stored until it is needed. As the deer feeds daily under the oak trees, eating every fallen acorn it can find, this high-energy food fills its bone marrow with firm white fat, and forms a thick layer of solid fat across its loins and rump. A soft insulating sheet of fat also appears beneath the animal's skin, and small amounts of fat form around its kidneys and in the body cavity. As winter progresses and food becomes more difficult to find, such fat reserves may keep the deer from starving during this stressful time. The buck also draws on fat reserves during the rut, when his single-minded pursuit of does often reduces his food intake.

Although deer normally move constantly while feeding, taking a bite here and there as they walk, exceptions to this behavior occur when choice food items are found. On many occasions deer have been seen eating ripe yucca seedpods after the flowers have dropped off. These soft, decomposing seedpods are located four to five feet above the ground at the tops of the yucca stalks. One feeding deer was observed coming into contact with the sharp-tipped yucca leaves as it stood up on its hind legs to reach the pods, but the spines did not stop it from feeding. It "walked" around each plant on its hind legs, eating almost all of the seed-pods present, before dropping down onto all four feet. Another deer was seen eating ripe agarita berries from two large bushes about four feet tall with crowns four feet in diameter. This deer spent more than an hour at these bushes, searching for every berry and nibbling them off.

By the end of summer, ground forage may begin to shrivel and die from the heat and lack of moisture. Since most fawns are by then about two to three months old, and they are supplementing their dwindling milk diet with low-growing weeds and brush, this can be an especially hard time for them. When this vegetation dies and the only available browse grows too high for them to reach, fawns often starve. This harsh thinning-out process is the natural way to keep the deer population in balance with its habitat.

To eat the various plants that will make up its diet, a whitetail fawn is born with eight teeth, called incisors, in the front of its bottom jaw. There are no front teeth in the top jaw, and none will ever grow there. The bottom front teeth, which soon become sharp and hard, are its cutting teeth. If the fawn nips its mother with them while nursing, the doe gives her young fawn a little kick to remind it to nurse more gently.

By the end of the fawn's second month, twelve premolars have joined the eight incisors. These new teeth, located three on each side in both the top and bottom jaws, are its milk teeth or baby teeth. The third milk tooth in line has three points, called cusps, on its surface, but the premolar that will replace it has only two cusps. The fourth tooth is the first permanent molar to come in. All of the milk teeth will be replaced with permanent premolars by the time the deer is about a year and a half old, and three permanent molars will have joined them in each jaw. The deer

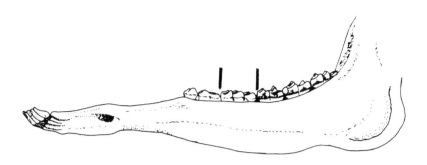

Jawbone of eighteen-month-old buck showing a three-cusp molar which will be replaced by a two-cusp molar. Illustration by Eugene Fuchs for Al Brothers and Murphy E. Ray, Jr., Producing Quality Whitetails *(Laredo, Tex., 1975).*

now has all of its teeth—eight incisors, twelve premolars, and twelve molars.

Having no front teeth in its upper jaw, a deer does not bite with teeth against teeth as many other animals do. Instead, its eight bottom teeth bite against a tough upper gum pad. Parts of tender plants are nibbled off with ease, but larger shoots and twigs may need to be bitten partway through, held firmly against the gum pad, and then jerked loose with a toss of the deer's head. Each mouthful does not have to be fully chewed; the deer merely breaks up the vegetation with a few chomps of its molars and then swallows. This method of eating allows the deer to fill its stomach quickly and then find a safe place to hide and finish digesting its food.

Plant cells contain a substance called cellulose, which most digestive systems are unable to break down and use for nutritional energy. Because a deer eats nothing but plant materials, it has a special digestive system to handle this type of food. Bacteria and protozoa living in the deer's stomach break down the cellulose, releasing the glucose it contains so that the deer's body can absorb and use the glucose. Without this help the deer could not survive on the type of vegetation it eats.

A complex four-chambered stomach is required for the digestive process. The first chamber is the rumen, which serves as a storage tank for the slightly chewed, quickly swallowed plants. When food is plentiful, a deer can fill its rumen in an hour, and it may not feed again for five or six hours. The rumen gently kneads the plant mixture while the bacteria and protozoa start breaking it down. There are millions of bacteria plus several hundred thousand protozoa in only a few drops of rumen fluid.

After the deer has eaten and found a safe place to bed down, it is ready to continue digesting its food in comfort. It returns a small portion of the plant mixture from the rumen to its mouth to be chewed. This regurgitated lump of food is called a cud, and animals that digest their food by chewing the cud are called ruminants. Cows, sheep, antelope, giraffes, and camels are other examples of ruminants. Studies have shown that a deer is least alert while it is ruminating. According to its brain wave patterns, it enters a condition almost like sleep. As it ruminates, the deer chews its cud slowly with powerful molars that have sharp ridges and furrows to shred and grind the tough plant fibers. When the cud has been chewed as many as fifty strokes, the deer swallows it once more.

This well-chewed cud now finds its way into the reticulum, the second stomach chamber. With the help of more bacteria and protozoa, the digestion process continues, and in an hour or two the finer parts of the mixture are ready to move into the third chamber, called the omasum. From here the food moves into the abomasum, which is the fourth and final chamber. As the plant mixture passes from the stomach through the small and large intestines, most of it has been converted into nutritional energy and absorbed into the deer's body. The remaining portion passes out of the large intestine as body waste and is left on

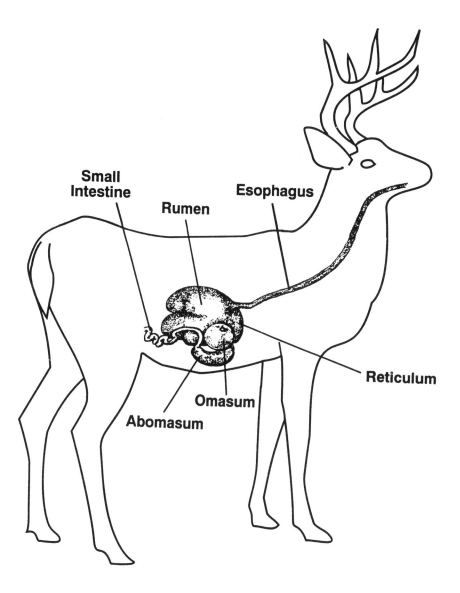

Four chambers comprise a deer's stomach. Food passes through each chamber before it is completely digested. Courtesy of Texas Agricultural Extension Service, Texas A&M University.

the ground in a pile of small pellets. The process from start to finish takes about twenty hours.

This daily chewing and grinding of food wears down the sharp ridges on the deer's molars. As the deer grows older, its teeth become smoother and its food becomes harder to chew. By the time the deer is eight or nine years old, its teeth may be worn to the gum line, and some may even be missing. An old deer with bad teeth cannot chew the tough, less desirable food that must be eaten when range conditions are poor. When its teeth can no longer process its food, the deer becomes weak and dies or falls prey to a predator.

Biologists can closely determine a white-tailed deer's age by counting its teeth, noting the tooth replacement sequence, and studying the amount of tooth wear on the molars in the lower jaw. Because the molars are usually wearing out by the eighth or ninth year, a deer in the wild seldom lives more than ten years.

All animals, including deer, must have a proper level of nutrition available throughout the year in order to maintain a healthy body condition and reproduce efficiently. The diet of a healthy whitetail should be 12 to 18 percent protein and have a calcium/phosphorous ratio of 2:1. These critical ingredients are hard to maintain and few habitats can provide this optimum level all year long. Deer can sustain themselves and reproduce on lower quality diets, but antler development and body growth will suffer and reproductive success will decrease dramatically. The first indication that habitat is declining in quality is a reduction of body weight in the various age classes and a decrease in the size of the bucks' antlers. There also will be a reduction in the average number of fawns per doe because fawn survival rates will be low. If the carrying capacity of the habitat is not exceeded, deaths due to malnutrition and starvation should not occur.

Appearance
and Sensory Mechanisms

Fossil records indicate that the white-tailed deer developed some fifteen to twenty million years ago during the Miocene age, and that its appearance has changed very little since that time. Sculptures, paintings, or photographs usually capture the male whitetail as he looks in the fall and winter. This is when the buck is at his best. His winter coat is a sleek grayish brown, and his polished antlers glisten in the sunlight. Thrashing the brush with his antlers, pushing and straining in head-to-head combat with other bucks, and carrying around the extra weight of his antlers have combined with the influence of sex hormones to develop large neck muscles that give him a more massive appearance during the breeding season. When he sheds his antlers in February or March, his neck muscles will return to normal size, and he may be mistaken for a doe until his new rack begins to grow.

The doe's long, slender neck tends to give her a more delicate appearance all year.

Having a moderately long neck allows the whitetail to browse on ground vegetation and still reach up to eat leaves off a tree. Without exposing its body, it can lift its head high enough to see over surrounding vegetation when checking and listening for approaching danger. These long, slender necks and the added height of the buck's antlers make whitetails look much larger than they really are. Shoulder heights range from twenty-six to forty-five inches, depending on the subspecies, and belly heights average about twenty inches from the ground. Bucks are slightly taller than does of the same age. Whitetails from the more arid habitats tend to have longer extremities, while eastern species have a more blocky appearance. If conditions are favorable, does reach their maximum weight in about four years, and males reach their peak in five to six years. Northern deer are usually larger than the ones found in the South, and a few of the average weights are: Ontario, 200 to 300 pounds; Wisconsin, 240; Kansas, 207; Louisiana, 130; Texas, 81 to 170; Panama, 80 to 120; Eastern Columbia, 66 to 110; Venezuela, 101; and Peru's coastal lowlands, 55 to 66. The heaviest buck recorded in Minnesota weighed 511 pounds, and New York's heaviest buck weighed 388 pounds. In South Texas, where many bucks with trophy antlers are found, a large buck may weigh 190 pounds.

Although differences in coloration, body sizes, and length of extremities do occur among white-tailed deer subspecies, only the most experienced taxonomist can separate them by their structural and genetic measurements. Crosses between subspecies have resulted from transplanting one into the range of another, further confusing the issue. The most reliable way to separate the subspecies is by cranial measurements and a new technology using mitochondrial DNA.

Lightweight tan to brown-colored hairs lying beneath slightly coarser, reddish guard hairs produce the reddish brown summer coat of the adult whitetail. The summer hairs are small in diameter and about half the length of the winter hairs. Little or no underfur is present in the summer coat, which allows free air movement to keep the deer's body cool in the heat. Unfortunately, the thin, lightweight summer hair may also give flies and mosquitoes access to the skin. Deer wear their summer coats for about three months in the northern part of their range and about four months elsewhere. Before winter arrives, the summer coat must be replaced with a warmer, heavier one. Because the grayish brown winter coat must grow from the same hair follicles, the summer hairs are crowded out one by one as the winter hairs emerge. This slow molting process starts at the neck and shoulders and then spreads to the rest of the deer's body. The belly and rump hairs are the last to be shed and replaced.

These new winter hairs are short and fine at first, but they grow longer and expand in diameter with time. As the hairs enlarge, their centers are filled with a pithy substance that helps insulate the deer from cold. By January the guard hairs may be two inches long, and they are crowded closely together to form a thick mat that warms the deer like a thermal blanket. A light growth of short underfur grows close to the skin and curls around the bases of the coarser guard hairs, providing additional warmth. The winter coat insulates the deer so well that its body heat does not melt snow landing on its back. The coat also keeps a whitetail warm when it must bed down in snow. The heavy winter coat sheds more quickly than the summer one because it loosens in large patches that are licked away by the deer's rough tongue during grooming.

The color of the coat may vary according to range, with the darkest colors appearing in the northern woodlands and the pal-

Because the deer's summer and winter coats grow from the same hair follicles, one coat must be shed as the other emerges. Courtesy Texas Parks and Wildlife Department.

est shades being found in the South. In the woodlands of its northern range, the whitetail's winter coat may appear to be a dark bluish gray, while its summer coat varies from brownish gray to reddish brown. The differences between the winter and summer coat coloration are less noticeable in southern whitetails. In the open brushlands of southwestern and western North America, the winter coat appears grayish brown, and the summer coat is brownish red. In subtropical and tropical habitats, the coat may have a more reddish color, and some tropical whitetail subspecies wear the reddish phase all year. Subspecies differences among South American whitetails may be revealed by the coloration of their winter coats.

Abnormally dark coloration in whitetails can be caused by an abundance of melanin, which is the black pigment of skin and hair. Melanism is genetically passed on, so it is possible to produce black white-tailed deer through selective breeding. Pinto-colored whitetails with large patches of white hair on their bodies also have been found. In some instances these deer have had more white than brown coloration. White deer occasionally appear during times of extreme drought, and researchers believe this is a temporary condition brought about by nutritional stress. These white deer are not albinos and do not have the characteristic pink eyes, nose, and feet that denote true albinism.

Although there are color variations from one habitat to another, one thing remains the same—a white-tailed deer from any part of the world is still recognizable as a white-tailed deer. In all seasons, the normal adult has a distinctive white band across its nose, white hair in its ears, and a noticeable white eye ring. Its chin is white with a black spot at each side near the mouth, and there is a large white patch at the throat that looks like a bib. The underparts of its body, including the insides of the legs, are also white.

A newborn fawn wears a rust-colored coat that may have as many as three hundred white spots, varying in size from a quarter-inch to a half-inch in diameter. The overall appearance resembles the dappled pattern sunlight and shade make when the sun shines through leaves. Camouflaged by its spotted coat, the fawn blends into its surroundings as it lies hidden in the vegetation. This spotted coat is shed in three or four months when the young deer grows its first winter coat. The male fawn can be distinguished from the female by the two "buttons" on his forehead. These small bony nubbins mark the spots from which his antlers will grow during his yearling spring and summer.

The whitetail is a strong, graceful animal designed for speed and agility, and it is the fastest member of the deer family. In the blink of an eye, a standing whitetail can be speeding away at thirty to thirty-five miles per hour, and it can stop and change direction in an instant. Running at top speed, it dodges trees, leaps small bushes, jumps over fences, and dashes through dense thickets. Long, powerful muscles in its slender legs are responsible for its running, leaping, and jumping abilities. They allow it to cover fifteen to twenty feet in a single bound or to jump a seven-foot fence with ease. The whitetail is also agile enough to go under or through a fence instead of jumping over it.

The feet of the whitetail are angled so that the deer runs on the tips of its two middle toes. They are covered by an extra thick toenail that is made of keratin, a substance that can be stronger than bone. These protective toenails on each foot have adapted to form the deer's sharp divided hooves. Their relatively small surface area enhances the animal's speed, traction, and maneuverability as it runs on its tiptoes. The springiness of the two-part hooves may even provide extra lift for its spectacular jumps.

Both the buck and doe have a large, conspicuous tail that averages about ten inches in length. The tail's white underside gives this deer its common name, but the animal is sometimes known as the "fantail" or "flagtail" deer in some regions. When a white-tailed deer is nervous or startled, it flips up its tail and holds it erect. As the frightened animal runs from danger, the uplifted tail becomes a warning flag to other nearby deer. Does are known to raise their tails more often than bucks when they are alarmed or when running away. Perhaps the doe's raised tail also serves as

As many as three hundred spots give the fawn's rust-colored coat a dappled appearance. Resembling the pattern sunlight and shade make when the sun shines through leaves, they allow it to blend into its surroundings. Courtesy Texas Parks and Wildlife Department.

a beacon to help her fawns follow her as she dashes away through dense vegetation.

Large, round eyes sit high and well to the sides of the deer's tapering head to give it a combination of monocular vision on each side and binocular vision to the front. Human peripheral vision covers 160 to 170 degrees, but when a deer looks straight ahead, it can detect motion in an area covering 300 to 310 degrees. This gives it a wide field of vision at a distance and allows the deer to see in every direction except directly behind itself. When it is looking straight ahead, its binocular vision only covers about 15 degrees, giving the deer a very limited field of binocular vision in close-up situations.

Vision is probably the poorest sense the deer has, but this does not mean that its eyesight is bad. It can see in both daylight and semidarkness, and its eyesight is specially adapted for seeing movement. Because motionless objects do not usually represent a danger in the deer's daily life, they are most often ignored. As a result, the deer will accept a person as part of the landscape if no smell or motion alerts it to the human's presence.

Another reason why a deer may ignore motionless objects could be related to the way it sees or does not see colors. Cones are the structures in human eyes that send color images to the brain. Deer lack these cones, so many researchers believe deer may also lack color vision, which would make their world appear in noncolors—white through all the shades of gray to black. Other researchers think whitetails may be able to see some colors, but that these colors may not look the same to deer as they do to people. Scientists may never know for sure.

Even if the deer is truly color-blind, it can still recognize in its surroundings things that do not belong. If a deer sees someone standing motionless in the woods wearing a bright yellow shirt and brown pants, the color of the pants will probably blend with the tree trunk colors and give no alarm. However, the yellow shirt may look like a light, bright blob where one does not belong, and its presence may send out a warning. On the other hand, if the shirt were green, it might blend in with the leaves and other background colors and go unnoticed. Observers have found that when a deer sees a large blob of solid color that is either too bright or too dark, it stares uneasily at the object. If the object remains motionless, the anxious deer will accept it as part of the surroundings until it moves. Hunters often wear camouflage materials to avoid appearing as solid blobs of color.

Because its eyesight is not always dependable, and its vision can be blocked by vegetation, a feeding deer depends more on sound than on sight to give the first warning of danger. Large ears set high on its head provide excellent hearing for the whitetail. Working like directional antennae, these ears can pinpoint the location of a sound as the deer turns them from side to side. By turning one ear forward and the other backward, the deer can listen for sounds ahead of it and still check its back trail for anything that may be following it. Hair in and around the ears help block out the wind noise and improve its hearing on windy days when sounds may be blurred. Hearing is well developed at birth, and the slightest noise will cause a fawn less than twelve hours old to snuggle closer to the ground and remain motionless.

A deer can hear another whitetail walking in heavy brush some fifty yards away; the noises we make while walking in the woods can probably be heard from even farther. The sounds of another deer's movements can be reassuring or they may serve as a warning. If the deer is moving at a normal pace, there is usually no cause for alarm, but a fast-moving deer is probably running away from something and the noises it makes alert the listening deer that possible danger may be approaching.

How does a deer decide which of the many sounds it hears mean danger? Each area has normal background noises and patterns of movement that have been learned and can be ignored. A nearby road produces traffic noises, but the deer knows that the sounds of moving cars and trucks are normal for that area. A car stopping by the side of the road may also be an acceptable noise;

however, the sounds of a car door opening and people getting out of the car may signal a warning to the deer.

Nature trails, picnic spots, and camping areas also have normal sounds and movements that are acceptable to nearby deer. People walking and talking on the established trails or busy with picnicking and camping activities at an established campsite may cause no alarm. Hikers on the trail may occasionally see a deer standing nearby feeding or cautiously watching them. Deer also may walk through a campsite, especially during the night or early morning hours. However, if a hiker or camper makes any movements toward the deer, it will be gone in a second.

Some deer hunters claim that a rhythmic sound, such as steady footsteps, will alarm a deer and that slow, intermittent sounds— a step, a pause, two casual steps, a pause, and so on—may not bother it. However, the sound of a breaking twig immediately brings a deer to full alert, whether the person who made the noise is walking intermittently or rhythmically. A low grunt or kissing sound will also bring deer to attention—body stiff, neck erect, eyes alert, and ears scanning the area for further sounds. If the person makes no additional noises, and is not seen or smelled, the deer may start eating again. Although it may appear relaxed, a feeding deer is always alert to its surroundings and ready to respond to danger.

Smell is another highly developed sense that may warn a deer of danger, lead it to food, help it find a mate, or allow it to communicate with another deer. A whitetail lives more by the messages it receives from its nose than by any other sense. As odors flood its system, the deer must sort them out and interpret the messages they are bringing. Most scents are carried in the air streams at about the same levels at which they were released. Obviously, the wind must be blowing in the right direction for the deer's nose to pick up these airborne scents.

A feeding deer's nose is full of the smells of the vegetation it is eating, so it must raise its head frequently to sniff the air for any odor indicating danger. With its moist, black nostrils twitching, the deer samples the air, building up a "picture of smells" with its nose. Any strange odor alerts the deer to be on guard and all of its senses are brought into use. Eyes search the surroundings for movement, ears scan the area for a sound that does not belong, and the nose tries to identify the scent. If no danger can be found, the nervous deer may begin to feed again; however, it remains alert and checks its surroundings frequently.

Strong winds, especially if blowing erratically, may mix the air currents and change the normal pattern of smells. It is hard for a deer to locate the source of a scent that comes and goes or changes direction. When strong winds interfere with the deer's hearing and change the normal movement patterns of trees and bushes, the whitetail's early warning systems break down. Branches thrashing in the wind create noise and confusion that may cause the disoriented animal to panic and run, or to remain standing too long to escape approaching danger. Observers have reported that deer often move into more open areas during periods of strong winds because the smells and sounds tend to be more directional in these open areas.

Because its nose gives the deer so many kinds of messages, it is not surprising that odors play a role in the deer's social life. Through its chemical communication system, a buck can tell when other deer are in the area. Bucks use their individual scent to mark the trees, bushes, and ground during the breeding season. The scent of a doe approaching breeding condition attracts the buck to her and tells him when she is ready. Body scent also allows the doe to recognize her fawn.

Four primary sets of skin glands on the whitetail's body secrete different scents, called pheromones, that can produce behavioral responses in other deer. The preorbital glands are located at the corners of each eye. In some species of deer the secretions of the preorbital glands are used to mark trees and bushes in the animal's home range, but in the white-tailed deer they are primarily tear glands that lubricate and cleanse its eyes. Although these glands secrete little or no scent, the buck still rubs them on branches and bushes in his area as if marking a territory. However, because the whitetail does not establish a territory to be defended against other deer, this rubbing may serve some other purpose.

The tarsal glands are found on the insides of the deer's hind legs at the heel joint, and they are a combination of oil and sweat glands that secrete an oily musk. Because adult deer of both sexes deliberately urinate on the gland's tufts of hair, an ammonia smell is also present. Why a deer wets on these glands is not clear, but researchers have learned that if the deer is unable to do so on the first attempt, it will try again every few minutes until it is successful. When excited, the deer raises the hairs of these tufts, and the tarsal glands emit a musk scent that mixes with the ammonia smell of the urine. As the hairs stand out at right angles to the skin, they appear to be pure white with no discernible urine stain.

Leaving an individual odor from the tarsal glands seems to be an instinctive action for deer. Within a week or ten days after birth, the fawn will try to hold its heels together and move its legs so that these glands will rub together. Keeping its balance while mastering the task is not always easy for the young fawn, and the doe encourages it by licking the glands whenever the fawn attempts to rub them together. When the fawn is a month old it begins wetting on its tarsal glands like the adults.

Researchers have discovered that bucks discharge the tarsal gland scent when they are in rut, and does use it to call or warn their fawns. Deer that have wandered away from their group release the scent like a call saying, "Where are you?" and members of the group respond with the scent message, "Here we are." All deer release the scent when frightened.

On the outside of the deer's hind legs between its ankle and hoof can be found the metatarsal glands. In black-tailed deer, the metatarsal scent signals alarm, but the function of these glands in whitetails has not been completely determined. Researchers do know that the glands secrete an oily substance with a strong, musk odor. These glands reach their largest size on species that gather in groups, and they are very small or absent on species that are solitary.

The fourth type of scent glands are the interdigital ones located between the toes on each foot. As the gland's surface is folded in upon itself, an inch-long, oblong sac is formed, which contains strong-smelling yellow waxy pellets. The skin inside the glands has a scattering of long hairs that transport the scent to the surface and deposit it between the hooves. Each step every deer takes leaves a scented footprint that may help individuals locate other members of their species or perhaps retrace their own steps. Because a frightened adult deer is able to leap fifteen to twenty feet in any direction while it is running, the few scent prints left behind during these giant leaps make it difficult for a predator to follow its trail.

A fourth sense—the sense of touch—is one that is sometimes overlooked in animals such as the deer. Instead of hands, the deer uses its mouth, tongue, and whiskers as tactile organs. Licking and nuzzling is an important part of the relationship between the doe and her young. It seems to bring satisfaction to the doe and is extremely important for the well-being of the fawn. It keeps the young one clean and helps remove odors that might attract a predator. Mutual grooming among adults has also been observed.

The uplifted tail is the ultimate signal of danger, and its white underside is highly visible as the deer bounds away to safety. Some people believe the doe's raised tail may also serve as a beacon to help her fawns follow her as she dashes through dense vegetation. Courtesy Texas Parks and Wildlife Department.

The deer's whiskers are located around its mouth and eyes, and as is the case with other whiskered animals, these strong bristles serve as feelers. Because the deer has very limited binocular vision in close-up situations, its whiskers help it to judge distance when feeding in scrub and brush. They also warn the deer when twigs, branches, and other objects are getting close to its eyes and mouth. As a result, it is very rare for a deer to suffer facial injuries caused by branches and twigs.

Deer are not the silent animals many people think they are. At least a dozen different sounds have been identified by researchers, and these may represent only part of the deer's vocal repertoire because some sounds may occur in a tone that is pitched too high for humans to hear. Deer have a variety of calls that are used in different situations. A fawn in distress bleats like a lamb for its mother, and the does "talk" to their fawns in guttural and mewing sounds. When deer become separated from one another, they may make a bleating contact call. All deer can make snorting noises by expelling air through their nostrils while their mouths are closed. These snorts are usually made when a deer senses danger but does not feel directly threatened. If a deer is being restrained or physically hurt, it makes a bawling sound.

A combination of body language and sound effects is used when danger threatens. A mildly disturbed deer often stamps its front feet, using only one foot or alternating between the two. Stamping, which may be a result of its agitation or an attempt to intimidate the unknown source of danger, may be accompanied by a snorting sound. If the threat of danger continues, the snort may turn into an explosive whistle that is expelled just before the deer bounds away. A startled deer may skip any or all of the preliminary signals, but displaying its uplifted tail with the highly visible white underside is the ultimate warning signal as it flees the area.

Antlers and Their Development

Horns and *antlers* are words that are sometimes mistakenly used interchangeably. Although horns and antlers are both growths that appear on the heads of various mammals, they are not alike. A horn has a bony center, or core, that is permanently attached to the animal's skull. A thin layer of skin covers this core and a tough outer layer of hardened keratin grows from its base. Keratin, which can be stronger than bone, is the substance also found in hooves, claws, fingernails, hair, snake skins, bird beaks, armadillo shells, and many other animal parts.

Hoofed animals in the *Bovidae* family, such as cattle, sheep, goats, and their wild relatives, grow horns. Both males and females may have them, but the female's horns are usually smaller and less impressive than the male's. Horns continue to grow throughout the animal's lifetime, and they can become an awesome sight. Some horns, like those of the bighorn sheep, grow in massive curving spirals. Others, like the gazelle's, may grow to a height of three feet, or they may span more than six feet, like the horns of the water buffalo.

The pronghorn antelope also has horns, but it has the distinction of being the only mammal that sheds part of its horns annually. A keratin sheath covers a bony core that is attached to the antelope's skull; however, a new sheath grows each year and pushes off the old one shortly after the breeding season ends. The male's horns are branched, or pronged, while the female's horns are smaller and seldom pronged.

Only members of the deer family, which includes deer, elk, moose, and caribou, can grow antlers. Unlike horns, antlers are a solid bone outgrowth of the animal's skeletal system. They grow from two permanent stumps of bone known as the pedicels, and they are composed of calcium, phosphorous, and other minerals. The most rapid deposit of bone material known in the animal kingdom occurs in antlers, and in some species, such as the caribou, the antlers may grow as much as an inch in two days.

Except among Chinese water deer and musk deer, all males in the deer family grow antlers of some kind or another. Antlers are used for fighting and in dominance displays between males. The buck with the biggest antlers is usually in prime condition, and he has no difficulty acquiring females and fending off lesser bucks during the breeding season.

Male Chinese water deer and musk deer have two long upper canine teeth that are used for fighting and showing dominance. Their canine teeth grow into sharp tusks about three inches long that extend below the lower jaw.

Antlers on female members of the deer family are not considered normal, except in the case of the caribou. Winter is a critical time for this species and all members of the herd must compete for the available food. Because the males shed their antlers after the rut, the females gain an advantage that allows them to get the nourishment they need while their unborn calves are developing. The females use their antlers throughout the harsh winter to shove other caribou away from the best feeding spots.

Moose can grow the largest antlers, which may measure some seven feet from tip to tip and weigh more than fifty pounds. Although the size of moose antlers can be quite impressive, the extinct Irish elk grew even bigger ones. One set of Irish elk antlers, found buried in a peat bog in Ireland, measured eleven feet from tip to tip, more than half again as wide as the antlers produced by the moose.

Even more amazing than the tremendous size of some of these antlers is the fact that members of the deer family shed them each year after the breeding season and grow a new set the next spring. This may seem like an extravagant waste of body tissue and nutritional energy; however, the shedding process allows the maturing animal to replace one year's antlers with a better set the following year. Also, if a deer damages its antlers, the accident is not a permanent handicap because the damaged set will be shed in the winter and replaced the following spring with an undamaged set.

Small swellings of antler growth are present on most male whitetail fawns by the time they are six months old, and until their antlers become more visible, these young whitetails are usually known as "button bucks." Since yearlings, like teenagers, require a lot of food energy to grow and develop healthy bodies, only the leftover energy can go into antler development. Consequently, a young buck's first set of antlers is usually small and may not have forks. However, when range conditions are good, yearlings with small six, eight, and even ten-point racks have occurred.

The size of any buck's antlers depends on his age, his genetics, and the amount of good quality food he eats while his antlers are growing. Between the buck's second and third years, his body growth slows and more of his food intake can be diverted to antler production. As a result, his second set of antlers usually is larger and has more tines (points) than his first. His third set should be even larger, and the shape of the rack he will grow for the rest of his lifetime becomes apparent—either wide, high, or basket-shaped. As he gets older, the main beams of his antlers may thicken, the spread may widen somewhat, his antler points may lengthen, and more points may appear, but the basic shape of his rack will remain the same. This shape as well as unusual characteristics such as drop tines, forked brow tines, or forked main points are hereditary.

The tines of the whitetail's antlers normally grow from one main beam, but occasionally a deer with a dichotomously branched rack will appear. The main beams of this abnormal rack divide and each portion forks into two tines like the antlers of a mule deer. Another abnormality produces a flattened main beam that resembles the palmated antlers of the moose. Whitetails also have been found with several spikes growing from each side of the skull, or with cauliflower-like growths of bone instead of the normal antler beams. These abnormalities are genetic and can be passed along to offspring if the buck manages to breed. Other antler deformities may be the result of severe body injuries. Researchers discovered that when a deer with normal antlers suffered a severe injury to his left hind leg, he produced a deformed antler on the right side of his head the following year.

Whitetails one and a half years old or older that produce antlers with no forks or points are known as spike bucks. Their poorly developed antlers may be due to a lack of good quality food in their diets, since a higher percentage of spike bucks appears in

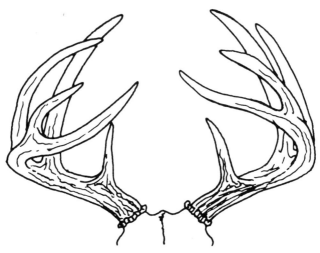

A buck's antler shape becomes apparent as development continues. These basket-shaped antlers are one of three classifications, the others being wide and high. Illustration by Eugene Fuchs for Al Brothers and Murphy E. Ray, Jr., Producing Quality Whitetails *(Laredo, Tex., 1975).*

years when an overpopulation of deer or unfavorable range conditions reduce the available food supply. Spike bucks can also be a result of genetics. Just as some people are not genetically programmed to be six feet tall, some bucks are not genetically programmed to grow trophy antlers regardless of how long they live or how much nutritious food they eat.

A buck's age cannot be determined by counting the tines on his antlers, but the size of his rack may provide a clue to his age. Trophy-type antlers usually appear in a buck's fourth year, primarily because body growth stops that year. The largest racks generally grow during the fifth and sixth years when the buck is in his prime. As he grows older, his body condition begins to deteriorate and the size and quality of his antlers also declines.

The annual growth cycle of a white-tailed deer's antlers begins soon after the old rack has been shed. Antler buds for the new rack start growing from the pedicels, two permanent stumps

A buck one and a half years old or older with only two hardened points protruding from its skull is a spike buck. Though a higher percentage appears when overpopulation or poor range conditions reduce the food supply, this development can also be hereditary. Courtesy Texas Parks and Wildlife Department.

of bone located on top of the buck's skull. A soft hairy skin, called "velvet," covers the antlers from the time they first appear as fuzzy knobs until they have reached full size. As the knobs grow in length, their velvet covering gives them a clublike appearance until the first fork appears. Growth is extremely fast, allowing the buck to produce his full rack in a few months. By May the antlers will be readily visible, and by August most racks have reached their full size.

Three complete sets of arteries provide nourishment for the rapidly growing antlers. One set is on the inside, carrying blood to the interior of the growing bone, while a second set is found on the outside beneath the velvet. The third set, located in the velvet skin, not only provides nourishment for the antlers but also acts as a cooling system for the deer. The maze of blood vessels in the velvet brings some of the animal's body heat to the surface where it can escape. Because the soft, growing antlers are full of nerves and blood vessels, they will bleed if they are cut or broken. A serious injury at this time could produce a deformed set.

From June to August, bucks may be seen gently rubbing their velvet-covered antlers against the insides of their hind legs, on their own necks, or on the necks of other deer. This rubbing is done carefully, as if the antlers are quite tender, and it seems to be aimed at relieving itching rather than as an attempt to remove the velvet covering.

In September the buck's complex hormone balance changes as his body gets ready for breeding. The blood supply to his antlers is shut down and the soft bone begins to harden beneath the velvet from the base to the tips. As the antlers harden, ridges formed at the base mark the former paths of the arteries. When the velvet loses its blood supply, it dries up and starts peeling away. It is not unusual to see a buck with shreds of dried velvet hanging from his antlers like Spanish moss from a tree limb during this time. Occasionally a buck eats the shreds of velvet from the antlers of another buck in his summer fraternal group. Does also have been seen nibbling hanging pieces of velvet from the racks of small bucks that may be their offspring. Rubbing the antlers on trees and bushes is a more common way to get rid of the velvet, and this process polishes the antlers as well.

By the first of October, 90 percent of the bucks will have bare, polished antlers, ranging in color from dark reddish brown to creamy yellow. The color is determined by the amount of staining from the blood in the velvet and from juices in the trees and plants upon which the antlers were rubbed. As time passes, moisture and sunlight usually bleach the antlers to a lighter color.

Hardening well before the breeding season starts, antlers provide a means for the bucks to establish a dominance hierarchy among themselves before they confront one another over does. These early sparring matches, called "push fights," help eliminate many battles during the actual rut, but spectacular hostile confrontations may still occur when opponents meet. Since the bucks' antlers are now solid calcium, no bleeding will occur if a tine breaks off during combat. Considering the tremendous impact on the tines during one of these body-jolting clashes, it is surprising that antlers break so seldom as the bucks thrash around.

The hormone testosterone keeps the antlers firmly attached to the buck's head; however, when the breeding season ends, production of this hormone stops. The bone at the base of each antler erodes or wears away, and the rack is ready to be shed. At this time the buck may be seen shaking his head back and forth in an attempt to dislodge the antlers. In his eagerness to be rid of them, he may rub them vigorously on a tree trunk or drop his head and plunge the tines into the ground, twisting his neck to break free of the rack. One side of the rack may be removed several days before the other side is shed.

Bucks shed their antlers from late December to late March, with most of the shedding occurring in February and March. Young bucks may be slower to drop their antlers than mature bucks, but once a buck is fully grown, he normally drops his antlers at the same time each year. Shedding times may vary from the north to the south, and in the Southern Hemisphere where seasons are reversed, antlers are shed during October and November.

When the buck sheds his antlers, a slight amount of blood oozes from the raw pedicels. If the antlers are broken off before the blood vessels have constricted properly, the pedicel may bleed more noticeably. Scabs quickly form, leaving only scars to mark the spots where the antlers were attached. Once the pedicels heal, new antler buds form, and the buck is ready to grow next year's rack. The buck's pituitary gland, stimulated by increasing hours of daylight, starts the growing process.

With so many sets of antlers being shed each year, why aren't more of them found lying around on the ground? They usually become food for mice, rats, squirrels, and porcupines. The calcium and phosphorous in an antler provide nourishment for the rodents nibbling away, and the gnawing action helps keep their teeth worn down. Antlers that are not found and eaten are bleached, softened, and weathered by the sun and rain until they become part of the soil. Their minerals may one day provide the soil nutrients to grow a plant that a buck will eat to provide nourishment for his growing antlers. So go the cycles of nature.

Occasionally a hormone imbalance will cause a whitetail doe to grow antlers. Her antlers are usually short spikes, and they may remain covered with a velvetlike skin at all times. She does not shed and replace them each year, and they may remain attached throughout her lifetime. Does have grown antlers when experimentally injected with the male hormone testosterone in the spring. An antlered doe is usually fertile, able to breed successfully and produce healthy fawns.

To avoid confusion during the hunting season, the term *antlered deer* is often used instead of *bucks* in game laws. This protects the hunter who sees a doe with antlers, thinks she is a buck, and mistakenly shoots her for a legal male deer.

In the late 1950s, another rare antler condition was found among Texas whitetail bucks living in the Central Mineral Basin (Llano, Mason, and Gillespie counties) where the soil was comprised of eroded granite, sandstone, gneiss, schist, and other igneous intrusions. These hypogonadal bucks, which became known as "velvet-horns," did not shed the velvet skin covering on their antlers as normal bucks do in the fall. Studies of these velvet-horns revealed that their testicles were quite small, and usually did not function, which might explain why their antlers remained in velvet. If a normal buck is castrated while his antlers are in velvet, his antlers will not harden or lose their velvet. If a normal buck with polished antlers is castrated, he will shed his antlers within a week. If a normal buck is castrated after shedding his antlers, the antlers will grow the next year, but the velvet will not be shed.

It was reported that a hard freeze one January caused the velvet at the tips of a velvet-horn's antlers to freeze and turn black within a few days. Because the antler tips could no longer receive a supply of warm blood through the damaged velvet, the soft living antlers froze and died. With time, the black velvet began to peel, but the velvet-horn made no attempt to rub it off on bushes or trees. Instead of shedding at the base as normal antlers do, the exposed dead portion rotted off at the freeze line, leaving the living base still attached. In late March, new antler growth began at the stub, producing an even more abnormal-looking rack.

The 1,318 velvet-horns harvested in this region during the 1959–62 hunting seasons were shot on granite gravel soil, or within a mile and a half of this type of soil. Because this distance is within the normal boundaries of a whitetail's home range, one theory is that the unusual condition may have been caused when deer ate a gonadotoxic plant growing in the granite gravel soil. Research was discontinued in 1967 when velvet-horns stopped occurring in the area, having added their touch of mystery to the annual miracle of antlers.

Reproduction

North American whitetail bucks are in breeding condition from late summer or early fall to late winter, and it is extremely rare to find an adult doe that has not been bred by at least one buck during this time. They are very successful breeders, and their reproduction rate is unusually high for such large mammals. Breeding condition in the buck is triggered by the length of the daylight period. As the days grow shorter near the end of summer, production of the male hormone testosterone increases, causing the buck's testicles to enlarge and begin producing mature sperm. The presence of this hormone also stops antler growth, causing the antlers to harden and shed their velvet covering.

In regions of South America with an equatorial climate, whitetail bucks may breed throughout the year, but most of the breeding activity in the Venezuelan subspecies takes place between February and August. These months include the dry season, when most of the older does are bred, and the first part of the wet season, when the younger does are bred. Because breeding is not seasonal, fawns can be born throughout the year, but heavy fawning is common from July to November during the rainy season. A second peak occurs during February and March, which is the dry season; however, the fawn crop born during the wet season is usually two to three times more numerous than the dry season fawn crop.

Competition between bucks increases with the onset of the breeding season as they establish a dominance hierarchy among themselves. Challenging each other to determine their rank during this season occurs most frequently after their antlers have hardened, but before the bucks enter the final stage of sexual excitement known as the rut. When one of two contending bucks is obviously larger than the other, a hard stare may be enough to end the challenge, but when the bucks are more evenly matched, a push-fight takes place. Bucks seldom display real animosity toward each other during this testing period before the rut, and the dominated one usually breaks off the encounter before a push-fight increases in intensity. Hostile antler fights are more common during the rut and they usually occur between two bucks that have not met and challenged each other earlier in the season, or when a subordinate commits the faux pas of coming between a more dominant buck and the doe that buck is courting. Does may or may not be present during hostile encounters between bucks.

The buck starts getting ready to breed weeks before the doe is willing to accept his attentions. During this waiting period he polishes his antlers, rubbing them on nearby bushes and trees. Small, flexible trees less than two inches in diameter are heavily utilized, and the bark may be knocked off two to three feet above the ground by his rubbing activities. Once a tree or bush has been "rubbed," the buck may or may not come back to rub it again; however, his activities must leave behind some of his body scent because does have been seen sniffing, licking, and even rubbing their own foreheads on the same vegetation. Rubs are usually more numerous near the buck's bedding ground.

To announce his presence in the area and perhaps attract a willing doe, the buck prepares one or more scent-laden scrapes. Using one or both of his front feet, he paws the ground under an overhanging branch of a tree or bush. While standing in the torn up ground at the scrape, he often chews on the twigs over his head and twists his antlers in the branches. He may appear to be fighting mock battles as he pulls down small horizontal tree limbs with his antlers or mouth and then hooks the branches sideways a few times before they spring back to their normal positions. He also occasionally rubs his face on an overhanging branch, perhaps merely scratching an itch or possibly leaving some of his body scent on the branch. To add more of his personal scent, the buck urinates on his tarsal glands while standing in the scraped area. He will return to his scrape many times during the breeding season to paw the ground, urinate, and leave more scent. By the end of the season, his scrape may be three or four inches deep and three or more feet square.

Because white-tailed deer do not defend a territory against other bucks or does, these rubs and scrapes are not used as territorial markings to warn off other deer. Instead they are considered deer "letter drops," where the buck can leave a message that he is in the area, which signals his dominance level and his readiness to breed, in case an interested doe wanders by. When a doe in or nearing her breeding cycle is attracted to one of these scent-laden scrapes, she also stops and urinates in it, leaving behind a message for the buck. It tells him of her presence in the area, indicates her breeding condition, and puts him on her trail.

When deer numbers are high and does are easy to find, the rubs and scrapes do not have as much social significance. At times like these, a buck searching for a doe merely inspects each group of females he encounters until he finds a doe approaching sexual receptivity. He follows her around, courting her until breeding has been accomplished, and then moves on to search for another doe.

People often wonder how many does one buck can breed in a season. The average number in the wild is probably less than ten, but under conditions controlled by researchers, one buck managed to breed thirty-two does. During one study in Texas, a wild buck bred six does during the season, and in each instance he courted the doe for a couple of days prior to breeding.

From October through January, all breeding-age bucks may participate in courtships, but not all of them get to breed a doe. At any time of the day, several bucks may be seen tirelessly pursuing a doe until she either eludes them or accepts the most dominant one as a mate. As the bucks trail along with their noses close to the ground following her scent, the dominant buck is in front leading the chase. The bucks may make low bleats, pants, or moaning sounds as they trail along behind her, and an occasional clicking sound can be heard if their hocks rub together as they walk. They follow her trail by scent until they get close enough to follow her by sight.

A buck becomes aware that a doe is about ready to breed by seeing other bucks chasing her or by catching her scent. Stretching his neck forward, the buck raises his nose in the air, curls back his upper lip, and sniffs the air. If a doe is scented, the prenuptial chase begins; however, the doe will not allow a buck to mount her until she is ready, and she runs hard to avoid being caught too soon. Moving in large circles or dashing away through the brush, she tries to get away, but the closer she is to sexual receptivity, the more persistent he becomes. She is absolutely receptive for only a few hours during her estrus cycle. In most cases courtship is more like persistent "hounding" than a chase. The male approaches and attempts to mount; she walks away—until finally at the propitious moment she stands and they copulate.

On one occasion an observer reported seeing a large buck chasing an extremely tired but unwilling doe. When the buck caught up with her, she dropped to the ground so that he could not mount her. Although she was not ready to receive him, he struck her with his front hooves until she got up, and then began chasing her again. Three times she was seen dropping to the ground and each time he prodded her until she got to her feet again. They were last seen entering the thick brush with him still pursuing her. The younger or less dominant bucks often have the opportunity to court a doe, but they are quickly displaced if a more dominant buck arrives on the scene. A large dominant buck will usually breed every receptive doe he courts during the rut. His presence keeps other bucks at a distance, but if he is challenged, the winner of the battle gets the doe. She does not seem to care which one wins, and the successful buck will mount her as often as possible during the short time she is sexually receptive.

When a buck catches up with a doe in heat, he may have to make only a few short dashes toward her before she accepts him. If she is not ready to breed, he may have to chase her for a while or court her for a day or so. He may be seen feeding and bedding down with a group of does, but he will be paying special attention to the one he is courting. He follows her wherever she goes and when she is finally ready to breed, she stops, spreads her hind legs a little, lowers her rump slightly, and holds her tail up or to one side. He will approach her and may begin licking around her tail while she stands motionless. He may strike her lightly on the side with one hoof and then resume licking her. If she continues to stand motionless with her legs spread, he mounts her, slowly climbing forward with his hooves. He may lick her neck and lay his neck beside hers for a few seconds before entering her. The force of his first thrust may separate them, and when this happens they often stand still for a minute or two before the doe begins feeding and moving away from him. He follows about ten yards behind her, occasionally feeding as he trails along. As time passes, his interest is rekindled and he approaches her again. Although she may run, causing him to have to chase or court her again, she will be receptive to his sexual attentions for about twenty-four hours. He may hang around for a few hours after she is no longer receptive, but when he is sure she will not allow him to mount her again, he departs to find another willing doe.

The adult buck is not part of a family unit. Although he and a particular doe may have mated, they do not become mates in the sense of a lasting bond being formed between them during their short courtship. If they ever meet again, there is no sign of recognition. The only thing that will attract him to her in the future is the scent of her heat cycle during another breeding season. She is solely responsible for the birth and survival of her fawn.

A combination of body condition, hormone levels, temperature, and the length of the daylight period prepares the doe's body for breeding. As she enters her first estrus cycle, commonly known as "coming into heat," she begins to urinate more frequently. Pheromones in her urine leave the chemical message that she is becoming ready to breed, and any buck that gets a whiff of this message will be hot on her trail. A doe usually conceives during her first estrus cycle, but if she fails to be bred or fails to conceive, she may come into heat again at twenty-five- to thirty-day intervals for up to three cycles. It is very rare to find a doe that has been overlooked by a rutting buck during the breeding season.

If conditions are right, an "early fawn" doe may breed her first fall and give birth to a fawn when she is only a year old. Otherwise, she will not breed until her second fall when she is about eighteen months old. A single fawn is usually the result of the first encounter, but a healthy doe normally gives birth to twin fawns each year from then on. The wild doe's reproductive rate starts to decline when she is six or seven years old, but captive does in research studies have continued to reproduce for as long as twelve to fifteen years.

Studies have shown that when range conditions are poor, a larger percentage of the fawns will be males, but when range conditions are extremely good, more female fawns appear. High-energy food studies with goats produced similar results, so this may be one of nature's ways to reduce the number of reproducing females when food is scarce and increase them in times of plenty. When range conditions are extremely poor and does are seriously undernourished, fawns may be born dead or in such a weakened condition that they do not survive. The amount of milk does can produce also decreases.

Because a doe has four teats, she could physically nurse four young, but it would be difficult for her to find enough high-quality food to maintain her own body and still produce the milk needed to feed this many fawns. High milk production is stressful, and even a well-fed doe will lose weight until her fawns are weaned. Quadruplets may occur in one out of a thousand births, and triplets in about one out of a hundred births, but survival rate is low.

In April or May, after a gestation period of about seven months (200 to 210 days), the doe is ready to give birth to a five- to seven-pound fawn. Male fawns are usually about a pound heavier than females. A pregnant doe normally lives in a matriarchal group consisting of an older doe, some of the older doe's fawns, and their fawns; she usually separates herself from the group to give birth. If she is the older doe, she may have to chase her offspring away to be alone, but if she is one of the offspring, she will wander away from her mother's group to have her first fawn. A doe rarely has serious problems giving birth, and the event will take place wherever she happens to be when her time arrives. Although no special place is chosen in advance, it is not unusual for a doe to return to the same area of her range each year to bear her fawns.

As soon as the fawn is born, the doe thoroughly cleans its spotted coat with her tongue, licking away all traces of the birth. The umbilical cord, which breaks as the fawn emerges, gets special attention as she licks its stub and then bites it off close to the fawn's body. Over the next few days, she cleans this spot often to prevent infection. During the fawn's first grooming, she may lick its body so vigorously that it is partially lifted off the ground, settling with a tiny thud after each tongue stroke. Her thorough cleaning leaves the fawn with very little scent of its own, which helps prevent it from being found by predators.

Getting some nourishment into the fawn is the next important step because this feeding must provide the newborn with the energy it needs to survive this first critical period. The doe's rich, warm milk contains more dry solids than cow's milk, and it may have as much as three times the fat and protein. It can double the fawn's body weight in about two weeks and triple it within a month. The doe may lie down for the first feeding if the newborn is so weak that it can barely lift its head, but she will not lie down for its future feedings. This means even an extremely weak fawn must gain enough energy from its first feeding to enable it to stand up and nurse from her udder the next time she comes to feed it.

The fawn vigorously wags its tail as it nurses, and the doe responds by licking its rear end, which stimulates its bodily functions and may prevent constipation. She also carefully licks the rest of its body to remove any odors the fawn may have picked up since its last grooming. The doe's scent does not concentrate around the newborn fawn because she visits it only for short periods to allow it to nurse. She returns three or four times a day during the first two weeks, but the number of visits gradually increases over the month that follows.

Because a newborn fawn's digestive system cannot process plant materials for a while, it is nourished only by its mother's milk. In a few weeks the fawn will start eating some plants, but it still needs milk to survive. The doe may allow it to continue nursing until the breeding season begins, but most fawns are weaned by the time they are four months old. The fawn also sheds its spotted coat about this time and could probably survive if something happened to the doe.

For the first few weeks of its life, the fawn is not strong enough to follow its mother and must bed down alone. Regardless of its age, the fawn seems to choose its own bedding site, and although twins tend to bed down separately, the doe brings them together for the nursing periods. If the fawn tries to follow the doe when she starts to leave, she may use her front foot or nose to push it down, reinforcing the message that it must stay by itself and remain hidden. When it is time for her to leave, she utters a soft guttural sound, and the fawn drops to the ground and hides in the vegetation. This usually places it in a new bedding location after each feeding. After the first few days, the fawn gets up, wanders around a bit while the doe is gone, and may bed down in still another spot. When its mother returns, she has to find it.

Interestingly, she cannot recognize her own fawn by sight, although later, members of matriarchal and fraternal groups seem to recognize one another by sight at a distance. As the doe approaches the area where she left her fawn, she walks along with her neck outstretched and her ears perked forward, making a soft, low sound. Hearing this feeding call, the fawn lifts its head above the grass and may respond with a mewing call or an anxious bleat.

If it is old enough, it jumps up and runs to meet her. She sniffs its scent to make sure it is her fawn and then allows it to nurse. When several young fawns are bedded down in the same general area, it is not uncommon for the wrong fawn to respond to a mother's feeding call. The youngster is quickly rejected when the doe does not recognize its scent as that of her own fawn.

During the fawn's second week it becomes more active, developing and strengthening its muscles by prancing and playing around after nursing. As it grows stronger, the fawn may run ten to twenty yards away from its mother, stop, and then dash back to her, sometimes dodging back and forth as it runs. The doe remains with her fawn for a few minutes after each feeding, eating and keeping watch while it engages in this playful activity.

By the time the fawn is six weeks old, it is following its mother around part of the time and being taught to look, listen, and eat some vegetation along the way. As it grows older, it accompanies her for greater distances and longer periods. By fall, the fawn is traveling everywhere with its mother, and it remains with her until April or May of the following year when she drives it away before giving birth again. It will be allowed to return to her matriarchal group after her new fawns are born.

A study of fawns and their survival rates revealed that during the first few days of its life, a fawn usually remains motionless when approached. Instinct tells the fawn to lie still, and its protective coloring helps it blend into the surroundings. If it does not move, it may not be seen. Coyotes often specialize in hunting for such immobile fawns when cover is sparse and other food is scarce. They can take at least half of the fawns in their hunting area during the fawns' first sixty days of life.

The instinct to lie still does not protect the fawn from people either. There is something irresistible about a little spotted fawn curled up in the grass. Perhaps it evokes Bambi memories, or per-

By fall, a fawn travels everywhere with its mother and remains with her until the next spring when she drives it away before giving birth again. Courtesy Texas Parks and Wildlife Department.

haps it simply triggers the response of wanting to help something that looks so helpless. Regardless of the motivation, taking a fawn from the wild is a violation of both state laws and the laws of nature. People tend to rationalize this crime by imagining that the fawn must have been abandoned by its mother and it is too weak to get up and run away. They assume the mother must be dead, and the fawn will die too if someone does not rescue it. The fawn is then bundled up and carried away to a nearby car.

In reality, the mother is probably close enough to hear and

smell the humans who have taken away her fawn. After they have gone, she returns to the area, walking along with her neck outstretched and her ears perked forward. Although she utters her soft feeding call, no little head rises above the vegetation in response. She walks a bit further, calling softly, and again nothing happens. She crisscrosses the entire area, searching for her missing fawn, and she will probably return several times during the next few days to look and call for it.

Many of the fawns thus "rescued" die of intestinal problems within the first few days of captivity because they do not get the proper food—the rich milk their mothers could provide. These fawns and the people who took them from the wild are the lucky ones because the fawns did not live long enough to cause legal problems and expenses for the kidnappers. There was not enough time for the fawn to earn its "rescuer" a game law violation and a hefty fine for taking it from the wild; or to cause a neighborhood dispute by eating someone's prized flowers or plants; or to slash a child's face with its sharp hooves; or to grow into a rutting, antlered buck capable of injuring or even killing someone. A "pet" deer can never be completely trusted because it will always be too wild for civilization. Moreover, after spending too much time with people, a deer becomes too civilized to survive very long in the wild. If the fawn is fortunate, neither a coyote nor a human will find it until it is old enough to get up and run fast enough to escape when approached. With luck it will survive and one day take its place in the courtship and breeding cycle of the white-tailed deer.

Social Behavior

All whitetails have a distance within which they will not tolerate another deer without resorting to some type of aggressive behavior. These aggressive interactions start when an individual deer's "space" is invaded, but the actual distance involved varies with the individual, season, and circumstances.

Social relationships among whitetails are well defined with the largest, strongest, and most aggressive bucks dominating the other males they associate with. To establish their social rank, they display several aggressive postures, each one a little stronger than the one before. The mildest display is the "ear drop." If the dominant buck drops his ears along his neck, his body language message tells the other deer to back off. The ear drop may be a strong enough message to send a challenger on his way. However, if the challenger stands his ground, the dominant buck gives him a "hard look." Standing stiff-legged with his ears flattened along his neck, he lowers his head slightly, extends his neck, and glares at the challenger. Direct eye contact is always considered an act of aggression, and the conflict will end at this point if the challenger turns his head and walks away.

If the challenger responds to the glare with a hard look of his own, the conflict progresses to the next stage and the dominant buck resorts to the "sidle." Turning his body about thirty degrees, he advances toward the challenger with stiff, sidling steps. His head is held high; his chin is tucked in; the hairs along his neck, back, hips, and rear legs are raised; and his tail is held tightly against his legs. The sideways approach and raised body hair make the buck look larger, increasing his chances of dominating his opponent.

Failure to yield to the sidle display brings on the "antler threat." The dominant buck drops his head and presents his polished antler points. If the challenger stands his ground and responds with his own antler threat, physical contact results. Before the rut begins, this contact will probably be a push-fight. The bucks walk slowly toward each other until their antlers make solid contact. Like sparring partners, they cautiously manipulate the antlers so that none of the tines come in contact with each other's skin. Then they begin pushing each other. No hostility is usually displayed, but they are putting all of their energy into the encounter because strength is the determining factor. When one buck is pushed back ten to twenty feet, he has clearly been dominated by a stronger buck. The loser usually breaks off contact, runs to one side, drops his head, and begins feeding as if nothing had happened. He is ignored by the victor.

Sometimes the antlers cannot be manipulated so that the tines do not touch the skin in a head-on push-fight. When this happens, the deer may position themselves so that their antlers make contact on the right or left side instead of head on. The outcome of such an encounter is not determined by the distance one pushes the other. The loser here is the buck that has had his head twisted closest to his neck.

Most push-fights occur between deer that have antlers quite similar in size. If there is a great difference in the size of the antlers on two bucks, the deer with the significantly smaller rack is probably also smaller in body size. More than likely he will yield to the larger buck before the challenge reaches the push-fight stage.

By the time breeding gets under way, each deer already knows which bucks he can dominate and which ones have made him back off. Establishing this dominance hierarchy before the bucks enter the rut helps reduce the number of hostile fights that take place when sexual activities are at their peak. Hostile fights that occur during the rut are usually between bucks that are strangers to each other. When does are scarce, bucks must wander out of their home ranges to find one, resulting in more hostile encounters between strangers. Most battles during the rut occur when a doe is being pursued, but they can take place whenever evenly matched bucks that have not had a chance to test each other happen to meet or when no decided victor resulted from their previous encounter.

Male hormone levels are high during the rut, and the bucks do not engage in mock battles or push fights. With heads lowered and antlers ready, they rush at each other with a body-jolting crash in an attempt to knock each other backward or sideways. They lock antlers and begin to shove and twist, kicking up clods of dirt and trampling the vegetation. Their encounters can be quite violent, but the bucks never deliberately fight to the death and they are usually reluctant to strike their opponent's flesh. If one of the bucks is knocked down, he is allowed to regain his footing before another rush takes place. The battle may end after a single violent rush or it may continue for twenty minutes or more. Few things will distract the bucks while they are fighting, and their combat does not end until one has had enough and gives way. The winner may be the challenger or the one that was challenged.

Occasionally the antlers get wedged so tightly together during a head-on rush that the bucks cannot separate no matter how much they twist and turn. When this happens, both bucks become losers because they cannot survive for long in this joined condition. Hunters sometimes discover the remains of two deer with their antlers still tightly locked together.

Sexually related hostility ends when the breeding season is over, but competition for food produces its share of aggressive behavior among deer. It is not uncommon for large numbers of deer to gather in open areas during feeding periods, and dominant deer of both sexes display aggressive behavior to get the best locations. A herd hierarchy is established by their interactions on the feeding grounds.

Like the buck, a doe displays the ear drop, hard look, and sidle as her first threat stages. She uses them within her family group, and her fawns follow her example to determine their own pecking order. When a doe establishes her dominance at a feeding area where more than one family group is present, she is doing it for herself. Her fawns may benefit from being close to her, but they can be challenged by her or by a deer from another group.

If there is a shortage of food, a doe may need to take more drastic steps to secure the best feeding area for herself. Because she has no antlers, she increases her threat display by lunging or rushing at her adversary and striking out with one or both front feet. If this kicking action does not win her dominance, a final stage of combat called "flailing" results. In this stage, both does stand up on their hind legs and slash at each other with their sharp front hooves. They do not bluff or fight mock battles and they do not strike each other lightly. Serious injuries may occur, and the flailing does not end until one doe has had enough and gives ground to the other. Fortunately, this type of conflict usually lasts only a few seconds.

Bucks also resort to kicking and flailing behavior when their antlers are missing or in velvet. Some observers believe the threat position of the deer's head when it makes eye contact with its opponent may signal its intentions. If the head is held low, it may indicate a readiness to chase or kick the opponent, but if the head is held high, it may signal a readiness to rear up and flail. Subordinate members of the herd quickly learn to avoid the more dominant deer on the feeding grounds, which reduces the number of conflicts and injuries that occur over food.

Fawns, both male and female, copy the aggressive behavior of their mothers. They quickly learn how to lay back their ears, give hard looks, sidle toward each other, lash out with their front feet, and rear up on their hind legs to strike at each other with their front hooves. Mock fights begin when the fawns are about three months old, teaching them the lessons in dominance they will need to take their place in the deer hierarchy.

In northern ranges where snow and severe weather are common, the deer get together and display a type of social behavior known as "yarding." This winter herd may gather in stream bottoms or along the edges of ponds, bogs, swamps, and lakes where evergreen trees provide shelter and browse plants such as white cedar, willows, and dogwood provide food. The ground under the evergreens has less snow than the ground under bare hardwoods in the same area, and the evergreen branches growing close to the ground help reduce wind and cold air flow, resulting in a warmer place for the deer to feed and bed down. These "yards" usually have a southern exposure to give deer the full benefit of the winter sun, and the deer return year after year to the same sites.

Deer remain in such yards throughout the winter season to conserve energy, and their arrival and departure times depend

A buck may resort to "flailing" to show dominance if a feeding dispute arises while his growing antlers are still in velvet. Courtesy Texas Parks and Wildlife Department.

on the severity of the weather. In northern Michigan, they may be confined to these yards for only twelve weeks during mild winters, but the time may extend to twenty weeks during severe winters.

In the struggle for survival, each deer is in competition with every other deer in the winter yard for food, and as more time passes, the conflicts increase. Biologists in Michigan studied one deer yard from February to late April one year and recorded the number of conflicts they observed between the deer. They discovered that the ear drop and hard look resolved more than a fourth of the encounters. Many others ended with the sidle, but some required more aggressive behavior.

Because none of the deer had antlers at this time of year, striking out at an opponent with one or both front feet usually settled a conflict. Only 4 percent of the confrontations progressed to the flailing stage, and most of these encounters took place between bucks. Flailing battles over food seemed to be more vicious and dangerous than the hostile battles fought between bucks during the rut. Flailing was rarely seen between a buck and doe or between two does during this particular study period, and it was not observed being used by an adult of either sex against a fawn.

According to the records, bucks challenged other bucks thirty-nine times, and they had to rush or strike out with their front feet in a little more than half of these challenges. Bucks challenged does eighty-four times, and they rushed or struck at does in more than half of the encounters. The most dominant deer in the yard were the three-year-old bucks, and the yearlings were the most submissive. Very old deer also ranked quite low in the hierarchy. Bucks were able to dominate all fawns and 80 percent of the does they confronted.

Does challenged other does on ninety-eight occasions, and two-thirds of these conflicts reached the rushing or striking stage. Does confronted fawns eighty-five times, and they rushed or struck at them at least three-fourths of the time. Fawns challenged other fawns twenty-eight times, and they rushed or struck out during more than three-fourths of the conflicts. Fawns challenged does four times, and the fawn actually struck out at the doe on three of the occasions. These were the acts of desperate fawns trying to survive as food became scarcer.

During the study, two does were observed staying very close to a particularly aggressive buck. He did not acknowledge or encourage their company, and he did not assist them in any way; however, just being close to him gave them a slight advantage in the competition for the best feeding site. A young buck stayed close to an aggressive, older doe for the same reason. These types of social attachments are usually temporary, but they can be advantageous while they last.

When the food supply in a winter yard is gone, people have tried to help the starving deer by attempting to drive them to another area where food is available. Unfortunately, such attempts usually fail because the deer do not want to leave their chosen yard. About the only thing that can be done to keep these deer alive until spring is to bring supplemental food into their wintering yard. When spring arrives with its abundant new growth of food, the winter herd separates into its smaller groups and leaves the wintering yard.

Studies have shown that bucks usually display four types of behavior patterns as they grow older, and each one determines the group in which they will be found.

An immature male stays with his mother for the first year of his life because he depends on her for survival. She may abandon him for a short time during the breeding season and chase him away later when she gives birth, but he can come back to her and her matriarchal group. In the fall, the group may contain his mother, a brother or sister, and the two new fawns born to his mother that year. If his sister was bred during her first season, she will be accompanied by her new fawn. Members of the family group are quite sociable, eating together and bedding down together, but the mother is usually the dominant deer in the group. If something happens to the mother, her offspring may remain together or they may join other family groups. Sometimes a young buck does not leave his family group until the summer when he is two years old. His home range during this stage of his life is usually limited to that of his mother.

During the first year of separation from his family group, a young buck becomes what is known as a "subdominant floater." He floats from group to group, but does not establish a permanent membership in any of them. He may spend some time in mixed groups containing both bucks and does, or he may run with groups of bucks only. Normally a buck of this age is not strong enough to become dominant in any group and he may remain a subdominant floater for a second year. His home range will be that of whatever group he is in at the time.

Because established membership in a group on a known home range confers many advantages favoring survival, these subdominant floaters live a precarious existence. They are the only deer in the herd that do not continuously partake of the advantages of group life. A high percentage of young bucks fail to survive the subdominant floater stage of life. Subdominant floaters are the means by which inbreeding is reduced in the herd. They may end up one to twenty-five miles from the matriarchal groups in which they grew up before becoming fraternal bucks.

Spring finds the bucks spending most of their time eating and growing a new set of soft, tender antlers that must not be used for combat. The breeding season is months away, and although they may be seen with does throughout the year, adult bucks tend to seek the companionship of other male deer at this time. Even though they usually are not related, these all-male sociable gatherings are called fraternal groups. A group may have more than sixteen members, or it can be as small as two bucks. Groups with more than seven males seem to be less stable than smaller groups, and gatherings of four to six bucks are more common.

The core membership of a fraternal group consists of two to four mature bucks with strong social bonds that provide stability for the group. The other males in the group are usually subdominant floaters that may come and go. Although aggression is lowest among the core animals, they still have a definite hier-

Adult bucks seek the companionship of other bucks in the spring when their growing antlers are in velvet. They form all-male gatherings called "fraternal groups" that normally break up during the rut. Courtesy Texas Parks and Wildlife Department.

archy based on size and strength. As in any group, the dominant deer can make the first claim to the choicest food or best location to bed down, and the younger floaters must yield to them. The core members tend to have a small home range and regular habits. Although these fraternal groups normally break up during the rut, the core members often get back together again when the breeding season is over.

The fourth behavior pattern is that of the "dominant floater." He is a large, mature buck that may be found in a mixed group, in a fraternal group, or with a group of does. He will have a high social ranking in any group he joins, and even though he is ranked the dominant deer in the group, he seldom spends much time with any one of them. His home range is usually quite large and he is often seen alone.

When the time to breed draws near, a buck no longer wants to spend his time with other males. He may be seen with a group of does or fawns, but most of the time he roams around by himself searching for a doe that is ready to receive his attentions. His behavior toward her is entirely sexual, and he actively seeks her company only when his nose tells him she is ready to breed. He may court her for a couple of days, but when she no longer accepts his attentions, he leaves her without a backward glance and their paths may never cross again. At the close of the breeding season the buck sheds his antlers, starts growing another set, and once again seeks the companionship of other male deer.

Abnormal bucks that kept their velvet-covered antlers all year added a new twist to the social behavior of deer in a portion of Texas in the late 1950s and early 1960s. These velvet-horns formed fraternal groups of three to seven bucks that stayed together throughout the year. They were very shy, and they approached normal deer with extreme caution, often standing apart and watching for as long as thirty minutes before venturing onto a feeding ground. They were always furtive, and with good reason, because their social rank was below that of all adult deer as well as some of the more aggressive yearlings and fawns. From March through August any conflicts with normal deer involved food, and these minor confrontations were quickly solved when the timid velvet-horns backed off. Their presence in a feeding area was tolerated as long as they kept their distance. When the velvet-horns felt threatened, they ran away without displaying any of the alarm signals used by normal deer.

The presence of velvet-horns was no longer tolerated when the breeding season arrived in September. Normal bucks became extremely aggressive and threatened them with polished antlers, even though the velvet-horns did not display any sexual behavior toward the does. It was not uncommon for a buck to charge a velvet-horn that was fifty to seventy-five yards away to keep it from approaching. One hunter reported seeing a velvet-horn being charged by a group of six normal bucks. They had slashed it with their hooves and hooked its rump bloody with their antlers before he arrived to put it out of its misery. A group attack on another deer is not normal behavior for white-tailed bucks during the breeding season or at any other time.

Grooming is a common activity within all of the deer social groups, and it can take place just before bedding down, just after rising, or during a "loafing" period. Young fawns are groomed by their mothers at each nursing session, and members of a family group occasionally spend time grooming one another's necks, heads, ears, or thighs. Mutual grooming is probably the only type of physical interaction between bucks that is not aggressive. Because a deer is able to reach every part of its own body with its mouth or hooves, self-grooming poses no problem.

At the end of the morning and evening feeding periods, the deer usually separate into their individual groups to bed down. Group members avoid facing one another, perhaps to avoid aggressive direct eye contact. Positioning themselves so as to look in different directions also helps them see any approaching danger. If the range is hilly, deer usually bed down in the higher elevations during the day and then move down into lower areas to feed and bed down at night. In more level terrain, the deer usually bed down in cover during the day and in open areas at night, sometimes remaining in the open to feed until midmorning.

Actual bedding time for a whitetail is probably less than two hours at a stretch, and the deer usually spends this time resting and chewing its cud. A deer may occasionally be seen lying with its head flat on the ground, and it may also curl up, tuck its nose

Self-grooming poses no problem for the whitetail because it is able to reach every part of its body with its mouth or hooves, but mutual grooming is a common activity within social groups. Courtesy Texas Parks and Wildlife Department.

into its flank, close its eyes, and go to sleep. True sleep seldom lasts more than a few minutes, and the deer is easily aroused.

Except for the aggressive displays learned from their mothers, the fawns' social behavior seems to revolve around running, jumping, and chasing one another. In large family groups, fawns may be seen playing alone or together. The youngest ones tend to play by themselves, paying little or no attention to the other fawns. Their activities seem to involve aimless running and jumping. They often run ten to twenty yards away from their mothers and then circle back, but if a young fawn runs thirty to forty yards off, its mother may run after it. When it is caught, she may lick it all over as if checking to be sure that it is unharmed.

Fawns begin to play together as they grow older, and games of tag are common throughout the summer. The fawn being chased runs in a large circle that may have a diameter of seventy-five yards, and the chasing fawns run in a slightly smaller circle. The pursuers do not seem to be trying to "catch" the running fawn. Instead, they are trying cut in front of it, as if becoming the leader is the object of the game. A fawn may also hide behind a bush, waiting for another fawn to run by so that it can jump out and try to get in front. Becoming the leader of the chase again appears to be the purpose of this activity.

Play serves the multiple functions of working off excess energy, exercising growing muscles, and preparing the young for situations they will face later. As the fawns run, jump, and become leaders of the chase, they are acquiring skills they will need as adults. They are learning how to escape from danger, how to leap over obstacles in their path, and perhaps preparing for the time they will be involved in mating chases.

Does also have been observed playing chase games with their older fawns. On one occasion a doe and her eleven-month-old fawn were seen chasing each other around a hundred-yard oval area. The fawn followed the doe about half of the distance, cutting in front of her as they rounded a curve. The doe then chased the fawn until they reached the other end of the oval, where she cut in front of the fawn to become leader again. This activity continued for about twelve minutes, with the two deer making twenty circuits.

Adult deer are not considered playful animals throughout their range, but they are occasionally seen running, jumping, and chasing each other in a wild and frisky manner. Are they just trying to avoid insects or some other unpleasant thing, or are these deer full of energy and kicking up their heels just for the fun of it? Some people believe adult playfulness indicates well-being, because undernourished deer would not have the energy to waste in such behavior. The following play incidents were observed on the Welder Wildlife Refuge in South Texas.

The first incident involved a group of twenty-four feeding deer. All of a sudden, one of the does jumped, bucked, threw her head in all directions, and ran wildly for fifteen to twenty yards. She then began chasing another doe. Her behavior seemed to be contagious because some of the other deer began jumping, bucking, and chasing one another. Soon all twenty-four deer were involved in the activity. The doe being chased ran at full speed with her neck low and outstretched, and the chasing doe stopped running about every ten yards to jump and buck. None of the deer attempted to leave the area, and annoying insects did not appear to be involved. Gradually the animals settled down and began feeding in the normal manner, but the wild behavior lasted for more than twenty minutes.

A second episode involved four bucks that were seen drinking at a water tank during August. One suddenly started running and bucking. Moving in circles, he threw up his head and twisted his body in the "sunfishing" movements of a rodeo bronco. He then ran directly at another buck and chased him in circles. The other two bucks joined in and all four ran in circles chasing one another. When the bucks stopped running, two of them carefully put their antlers together and gently pushed each other for about three minutes. All four bucks then left the watering area and resumed feeding.

The third incident took place as an electrical storm was approaching during September. It involved a buck, five does, and two fawns. All of them were seen running in circles twenty-five to thirty yards in diameter, chasing one another and being chased. Most of them jumped and bucked when approached by another running deer.

Whether or not such behavior classifies as play, this kind of exuberance will be long remembered by anyone fortunate enough to see it.

Mortality, Parasites, and Diseases

Evolving in an environment subject to frequent disturbances, such as by fire, has given the white-tailed deer the ability to adapt to a wide range of transitory and unstable conditions within its living area. These deer are such successful reproducers that their population often exceeds the carrying capacity of their habitat, which results in not enough food to go around. When deer numbers are high and adverse weather conditions arise, major die-offs can occur. Survival conditions are especially critical for the very young and very old deer when long periods of drought in the late summer and fall severely limit the amount of ground vegetation available. Young deer cannot reach the twigs and branches growing above their heads that must serve as food, and the teeth of old deer cannot chew and process this less desirable browse. Winter and its limited food supply is also hard on these two age classes, for the same reasons. In addition, the youngest and oldest deer rank so low in the herd hierarchy that they must yield to more dominant deer for whatever food is available. Starvation can take a heavy toll from both of these age groups during any long period of adverse weather.

Predation by coyotes and bobcats is another common cause of fawn mortality. In one three-year study, twenty fawns were captured and fitted with color-coded collars and radio transmitters. They were located daily during the first month and every third day for a second month. At the end of the second month the survivors were captured and their transmitters were removed. The first year, five fawns were killed by predators, five died from diseases or starvation, and ten managed to survive through their second month. Since severe drought conditions existed during the second year of the study, fawn mortality was much higher. Fourteen of the fawns fell to predators, perhaps due to the reduced vegetation in which to hide. Another four died of diseases or starvation, and only two lived through their second month. During this same drought period, more than half the adult deer in the study area were lost to starvation or diseases. Range conditions improved during the third year of the study and only two fawns were lost to predators. Thirteen were still alive at the end of the second month, but five had died of disease or starvation.

Fire ants in southern states can also contribute to fawn mortality when they swarm over a newborn whitetail. As the fawn tries to lick them off, it ends up being stung internally, including in the stomach, where autopsies have revealed fire ants in the hundreds. Blinded fawns, their eyes white from fire ant stings, have been found in the multiqueen mound areas in Texas. During a joint study conducted in 1991 by the U.S. Department of Agriculture, Texas Department of Agriculture, and Texas Tech University in Lubbock, researchers marked off ten parcels of land four hundred to six hundred acres in size. After grouping these parcels into five pairs, they treated one parcel in each pair with insecticide and left the other in its natural state. Although there was little difference between the wildlife populations in the paired parcels in the beginning, time told a different story. The following year there were twice as many quail and deer fawns in the treated areas and 90 percent less fire ants. Other studies are being conducted on fire ants and the data is beginning to come in, but it may be a while before results show what impact the fire ant invasion is having on the food chain and the wildlife community as a whole.

When deer are in good physical condition they can serve as hosts for many external parasites, such as ticks, lice, fleas, keds, and flies, with little ill effect. However, when deer numbers are high, food is scarce, and the animals are already in a weakened condition, these parasites become a secondary factor that can have a definite impact on survival in adults and can cause high fawn mortality. Ticks can be found on all deer throughout the spring and summer months, and they are commonly located around the ears and eyes, under the shoulders, and at the base of the buck's developing antlers, where an abundant blood supply is available. These sensitive areas are not easily scratched, so the ticks are seldom removed. Heavy tick infestations around the eyes of fawns may result in blindness or a secondary infection that saps their strength.

The female tick lays thousands of eggs after mating, and ticks can survive more than a year without feeding. After hatching from eggs, deer ticks go through three stages of development. The first stage, the larvae, usually attach themselves to small wild animals, especially rodents and birds. After feeding for several days or weeks, the larvae drop off the host, digest their blood meal, and molt into nymphs. They then attach themselves to rodents and other animals, including humans; feed again; drop off; molt; and become adults. The adults climb into the vegetation and catch a ride on a white-tailed deer, other large animal, or a person brushing by. Ticks do not leap onto the host animal. Instead, they use their hind legs to cling to the passing hosts and then crawl to a suitable spot to attach themselves to the skin. The scalp, back of the neck, underarms, waist, and groin are choice locations on humans.

Healthy adult deer are usually able to withstand the impact of these blood-sucking parasites; however, people who tramp around in areas frequented by deer and other host mammals may wind up hosting a few ticks themselves. There is a chance they also could be infected by diseases transmitted by these ticks. Rocky Mountain spotted fever and Lyme disease are the most common tick-borne diseases affecting humans. Studies conducted by the Texas Department of Health during the 1991–92 deer hunting season showed that less than 1 percent of the ticks they examined carried the Lyme disease and less than 10 percent carried Rocky Mountain spotted fever bacteria.

Lyme bacteria were found in the common black-legged deer tick, Lone Star tick, brown dog tick, and rabbit tick. As regards people infected, the study reported that Rocky Mountain spotted fever affects from 19 to 108 people annually, and from 33 to 82 people are treated for Lyme disease each year in Texas. Lyme disease has been reported in at least forty-three states, but it is most common in northeastern coastal states. The symptoms and severity of this disease can vary greatly, but in 50 percent of the cases a red, round-shaped rash appears within a month of the bite, spreading outward from the site and sometimes reaching a foot or more in diameter. Later stages of the disease become harder to diagnose since it mimics other illnesses. Some victims develop minor fever, aches, and pains, all symptoms similar to those in a mild case of flu. Others may suffer joint inflammation and pain like that in rheumatoid arthritis. Nervous system damage in some cases may cause loss of memory and of muscular coordination; headaches; depression; and facial paralysis resembling the symptoms of diseases such as meningitis and multiple sclerosis. The bacteria can even attack the heart. Fortunately, Lyme disease is treatable with antibiotics and is rarely fatal.

Preventing deer ticks from becoming attached is the best way to avoid any tick-borne diseases. Wearing light-colored clothing makes ticks easier to see while they are still crawling around. Tucking pant legs into boots or socks and using an approved insect repellent are also good preventive measures. Attached ticks should be removed promptly, and a doctor should be consulted if any illness with fever develops after exposure to ticks. Treatments for tick-borne diseases are most successful when antibiotics are started early.

Tularemia, commonly known as rabbit fever, is transmitted to animals by the bites of flies, fleas, ticks, and lice. Although small mammals, especially rabbits, are more likely to be infected, deer can also carry the disease. Tularemia is usually transmitted to people when small cuts or abrasions on the hands come in contact with the diseased animal while handling or field dressing it. The liver of an infected animal will be covered with white spots. Human symptoms include inflammation of the lymph glands and ulcers appearing at the infected point of contact. Headaches, chills, and a rapid rise of temperature are secondary symptoms. To cut down on the chances of infection, individuals should follow the normal rules of hygiene and wash their hands thoroughly to remove blood and other foreign matter as soon as possible after contact.

In addition to ticks, midsummer may find the deer's hair full of keds, parasitic flies that are present in both winged and wingless forms. Keds are the most prevalent and active external parasites found on deer, and they are easily seen slipping in a sideways movement among the hair. These blood-sucking parasites are often called crabs, cooties, and ticks, but they do not engorge themselves with blood to the point of extension as true ticks do. Studies in South Texas found keds on 64 percent of the deer examined, with the heaviest concentrations on deer from dense vegetation or sandy soil sites.

Lice, although tiny in size, may be found in concentrations large enough to be mistaken for dirt accumulations around the bases of the deer's hair. One of the least common external parasites found on deer is the javelina flea. Although South Texas deer are thought to be only an accidental and temporary host for them, these fleas have been found on as many as 14 percent of the deer examined in some areas where javelina are common.

Internal parasites put additional stress on deer, and one of the deadliest can be a parasitic infection called theileriasis. After entering the whitetail's blood stream through the bite of a tick, this microscopic blood parasite invades and destroys the red blood cells. Some of the parasites reproduce, and soon there are thousands more to invade and destroy additional red blood cells. Many deer carry *Theileria* organisms in their systems, but no ill effects are evident until the nutritional quality of the range begins to deteriorate. When the amount and quality of the food taken in drops below what is required to replace destroyed red blood cells, the deer becomes severely anemic. As its body condition deteriorates, walking becomes difficult, and the deer pays little attention to its surroundings as it continues to search for food. When its energy reserves are depleted the deer collapses, quickly dehydrates, and dies with little struggle.

Liver flukes are another internal parasite common to deer living in river bottoms and wet coastal prairies. These giant flat worms appear as swellings in the liver that can be felt as soft spots. They produce a black pigment that stains the liver as they devour it. When these dark areas are cut open, a dirty fluid pours out and one to four flukes will be found in the resulting cavity. The presence of these flukes is commonly called liver rot, and an infected liver should never be eaten.

Because the life cycle of the liver fluke requires the eggs and larvae to pass through water snails before entering white-tailed deer, cattle, or sheep, conditions must be just right for this parasite to develop. Its eggs must drop in water, the water must contain the right species of snails, vegetation for the host must be present, and the host must ingest the dormant liver flukes with the vegetation.

Sexual reproduction of this parasite takes place in the deer or other host mammal. Each liver fluke is a combination of both male and female and produces fertilized eggs that are discharged from its body in an intermittent stream as long as the fluke lives. The eggs move into the deer's intestine from the bile duct and are discharged with its intestinal waste. When this waste falls into water, the fluke eggs hatch into fuzzy microscopic creatures called miracidia that can track down a host water snail like a dog trailing a rabbit. Once the snail is found, the miracidia work their way into the soft skin, settling down in the tissues in or close to the snail's primitive lung. There they change into a saclike state called a sporocyst, which contains the cells capable of reproducing the next generation, known as rediae. The resulting rediae then break through the wall of the sporocyst and move into the snail's liver to produce a generation of tadpolelike creatures called cercariae. One miracidium can be responsible for producing three hundred cercariae. The free-swimming cercariae escape the snail and attach themselves to water plants by means of a sticky secretion. They develop a tough cystlike coating over their bodies and go into a dormant stage. As long as they remain moist, they will stay alive until the plant is eaten by a deer or other mammal. When they enter the intestine of the host, the young flukes emerge, burrow through the intestinal lining, enter the body cavity, invade the liver, and become established to complete the life cycle.

Setaria are long, white worms with bodies about the size of a paper clip wire. They may be found squirming around on the surface of the deer's intestines, and although they do little harm to the deer, they are not a welcome sight to a hunter field dressing a deer. Because these parasites are removed with the viscera, they do not harm the venison. Bladder worms, which are the larval form of the tapeworm, may also be found attached near or on the deer's liver in whitish bags of clear fluid with a whitish spot on one side. Infected livers should not be eaten by humans. Mature tapeworms are found in coyotes and bobcats, and when the eggs they expel on vegetation are eaten by deer, the eggs develop into the bladder worms. The life cycle continues when coyotes and bobcats eat a dead deer's viscera and become infected with new tapeworm larvae.

The pharyngeal botfly, more commonly called the throat bot, is an internal parasite deposited in egg form in the deer's nostrils in late summer or early fall. Adult deer strike out at the parent flies with their forefeet, try to run away from them, or hide their noses in the grass or in rodent holes to prevent the flies from laying their eggs. The throat bot completes its six-month life cycle during the fall and winter months and normally hangs at the back of the deer's throat. They must be quite an irritation because deer with throat bots may sneeze quite often. When the body temperature of the deer is reduced, such as when its carcass is put in cold storage by a hunter, the grublike bot works its way up the throat passage into the nasal or oral passage where it can be seen.

It can be a most unappetizing sight for someone anticipating a meal of venison, but its presence is not considered harmful to a healthy living deer or the venison.

Bacterial and viral diseases also affect deer survival, and one of the fatal ones, found throughout the United States and Canada, is anthrax. This bacterial disease, also known as charbon, does not occur often in deer, but it can be devastating in areas where there is an overpopulation of deer. The body wastes of a diseased animal or its carcass can contaminate the soil and water, allowing other deer to pick up the anthrax infection when feeding or drinking in these areas. As the disease progresses, an infected deer loses its coordination, staggers, and becomes stiff-legged. It may also have a bloody discharge from its nose and anus, and usually dies within forty-eight hours. Humans can be infected by anthrax when handling a diseased deer.

Epizootic hemorrhagic disease, commonly known as EHD, is one of the fatal viral diseases that deer get. Unlike anthrax, it is not passed from one diseased deer to another. Instead, it is transmitted by insects, such as blood-sucking gnats. An infected deer salivates excessively, runs a temperature, has a rapid heartbeat, and exhibits labored breathing. Its urine and saliva are often tinged with blood, and no internal organ is exempt from hemorrhaging as the disease affects the heart, liver, spleen, lungs, and intestinal tract. The deer loses its appetite, grows weak from lack of food, eventually becomes unconscious, and dies.

EHD usually appears in the late summer and early fall and can cause major die-offs in a deer herd. The first documented outbreak occurred in New Jersey in 1955, killing some seven hundred deer. Scattered outbreaks of EHD were found throughout the southeastern United States in 1971, and thousands of whitetails died in Nebraska, Wyoming, Kansas, and the Dakotas in 1976. Another thousand deer also died in New Jersey that same year. Annual outbreaks seem to be common in South Dakota, but EHD can appear anywhere on the continent if conditions are right.

Skin tumors are the most obvious disease deer have, and these tumors can be found on any part of its body. The virus that causes them is transmitted by insects and contaminated vegetation, and it can be spread when a healthy deer comes into direct contact with an infected deer. Humans cannot catch the deer tumor virus.

When discussing the impacts various factors have on white-tailed deer survival, human actions also need to be figured into the equation because of the obvious results of civilization. For example, by removing from many portions of the whitetail's range the large wild predators that would normally feed on deer, people have made it possible for deer numbers to increase dramatically. In areas where wolves, cougars, bobcats, coyotes, and bears remain, these wild predators still take a share of the deer each year. This natural culling process helps keep the deer population under control, but it is no longer adequate throughout the whitetail's range.

Other predators, such as unwanted dogs that have survived being dumped along country roads, often form packs and prey on deer. In the spring when they are heavy with unborn fawns and unable to run as fast as usual, does are especially vulnerable to dogs. Pet dogs that are allowed to roam free in deer country also band together in packs, often harassing, injuring, and sometimes killing deer. Dogs can be considered a significant problem, or just another way to keep the deer population in check, depending on the numbers of deer and dogs involved and on one's point of view.

Hunters have replaced the natural wild predators in most of the whitetail's range, and they legally harvest a small portion of the population each year. Legal hunting is carefully controlled by seasons and bag limits to make sure that the number of deer killed annually does not have a negative impact the whitetail population. Hunters remove about 10 to 12 percent of the deer population each year, but biologists estimate that the annual harvest could probably be increased to 20 percent in some areas without compromising a healthy population. Deer harvested legally by hunters in the fall can usually be replaced by fawns born the following spring if range conditions are suitable. Deer numbers in any given state are estimated from surveys, and in many regions deer are much more numerous today than they once were. Hunting licenses are issued with a percentage of the harvest in view. Yet even when wildlife managers consider a particular population too high for an area to support, the public view is often that there is still a shortage of deer.

Growing numbers of deer are hit and killed by automobiles and trucks each year, and as the highway system throughout the nation expands and the amount of traffic increases, these road kills will continue to multiply. Although fewer deer die on the highways in less populated states, road kills often exceed the legal harvest of deer in states with a high human population. Pennsylvania has reported as many as twenty-five thousand deer killed by cars in a single year within its borders, and Connecticut road kills often exceed the legal harvest in that state. Since the 1980s, between eight and ten thousand deer have been killed on New Jersey highways each year.

As the human population continues to expand and its need for space increases, deer numbers may not be able to remain at today's high levels. However, since the white-tailed deer is the nation's most popular big game animal, it should continue to receive special attention from professional game managers and wildlife agencies. They will make every effort to ensure that the deer survives in numbers great enough to provide food and recreational pleasure for hunters and nonhunters alike.

The white-tailed deer can also be counted on to do its part. As long as it can find enough food, water, and suitable cover to meet its needs, the deer will continue to reproduce in numbers greater than its habitat can support.

Historic and Economic Importance

The importance of white-tailed deer to people in North America has been enormous. Because of the animal's abundance and wide range, it has been used in almost every conceivable way, with the nature of uses shifting over time and doubtless destined to shift again in the future. From the earliest encounters between white-tails and the continent's first human arrivals, each change in human customs and settlement patterns has brought changes in how people view and use deer. These factors have always been determined by human wants and needs at any given time in history. A resource that appears to be abundant is often exploited, and the white-tailed deer was no exception.

Early European explorers and settlers in North America had never seen the white-tailed deer, but they were familiar with other deer species native to their homelands and they were quick to appreciate its potential. Historical writings make frequent references to the abundance of deer in the New World. For example, Thomas Morton, who chronicled the settlement of New England in 1632, noted: "The most usefull and most beneficiall beast which is bredd in those parts . . . is the Deare. There are in the Country three kindes of Deare of which there are great plenty."

Father Andrew White, a Catholic priest who settled in Maryland in 1634, wrote that whitetails were so plentiful "that they are rather an annoyance than an advantage." And in 1682 Thomas Ashe wrote of Carolina: "There is such infinite Herds [of whitetailed deer] that the whole country seems but one continued park."

Deer were viewed as among the most important animals in frontier America because they were a handy source of food, their hides could be made into clothing, and they were so abundant that they could be hunted all year. In a travelogue on the Southwest prepared for prospective pioneers, Captain Randolph Marcy wrote: "In passing through Southern Texas in 1846, thousands of deer were met daily, and as astonishing as it may appear, it was no uncommon spectacle to see from one to two hundred in a single herd; the prairies seemed literally alive with them."

It is estimated that there were thirty to forty million whitetailed deer on their historic range, which covered about three million square miles of North America in 1500. This estimate is based on there being a minimum of ten deer per square mile, with even greater numbers on portions of the range. Some researchers use the more conservative estimate of twenty-three to thirty-four million whitetails in the historic population. More than two million American Indians shared this range, and many of the tribes had been using the deer as a food source long before white settlement. Deer were as important to the American Indians of the eastern woodlands as bison became to the Plains Indians. Long before their interest focused on the buffalo, the relocating Plains Indians relied on the deer. Bison, moose, elk, deer, and black bear were found in many of the same areas as deer, but the whitetail was the most reliable and widespread source of meat for the American Indians, and they harvested between four and six million of them annually. In the Sioux language, the word for white-tailed deer is *tahca*, which means "the true meat" or "the real meat." Because fresh venison would not keep very long, the meat was often dried as jerky or used to make pemmican. Thus preserved, it could be stored for longer periods.

The whitetail provided more than just meat, however. American Indians found uses for every part of the deer. From antlers they fashioned arrowheads, spear and harpoon points, knife handles, needles, beads, whistles, and many household items. A club was considered a more powerful weapon when antler points were attached to it, and antlers also were used on ceremonial masks and as decorations.

The marrow in the leg bones was a favorite food, but the bones themselves were put to good use as clubs, hoes, digging sticks, and scrapers. Other bones were used to make eating utensils, fishhooks, needles, bracelets, beads, and other articles.

Deer hides were highly prized because clothing made from buckskin was so durable. Unlike buffalo, bear, and elk skins, which became stiff after being soaked in water, buckskin clothes remained soft enough to wear. Indian leggings, breechcloths, shirts, robes, shawls, dresses, skirts, sashes, headgear, moccasins, and mittens were commonly made of buckskin. It is reported that among seventeenth-century Huron Indians, a man needed the hides from at least six whitetails for his winter clothing, and eight hides were needed for a woman's winter clothes. Based on their population at that time, the Huron Indians probably used at least sixty-two thousand deer hides to make one set of winter clothing for each adult. Blankets, tepee coverings, mats, rugs, shield covers, quivers, wrapping for bows, storage bags, pouches, straps, and thongs were among the numerous uses of the versatile deer hides.

Before the coming of whites, the number of deer that people killed each year was based on need. There was no reason to kill more deer than a tribe needed for food and hides. Circumstances changed significantly when deer hides became a trade item for American Indians to exchange with the newcomers. Because of the abundance of deer and the quality of the hide, the whitetail played a major role in early American fur trading. When the commercial trade in deer hides reached its peak in the 1700s, the best buckskins were being sent to England, the next best hides went to Germany, and the least desirable hides were used within the colonies. Deer hides shipped from St. Louis and other trade centers farther north were more valuable than those shipped from the South because northern deer were usually larger. The high humidity in the South could also cause baled hides to rot during storage or while being transported. Hides dressed by the Indians were valued at five to six shillings per pound, and oil-tanned hides sold for a little more than seven shillings per pound. The value of an English shilling in the colonies varied. Some accounts say it was worth 24.3 cents while others cut its value in half, requiring two shillings to equal the twenty-five-cent silver piece.

Considering the small number of people involved in gathering them, it is astounding how many deer hides were exported. However, a single trapper might bring in more than a thousand deer hides at a time. Historical records show that from 1698 to 1715, two trade centers in Virginia and Carolina shipped more than a million hides. Another 5.5 million hides were shipped from South Carolina from 1715 to 1773. These 6.5 million hides do not represent the total deer harvest during this sixty-seven-year period. They are merely the number of deer hides shipped from a few trade centers in two states involved in the fur trading business. As the settlement frontier moved westward, one Texas trader baled and shipped at least seventy-five thousand deer hides from 1844 to 1853. His operation was located at Trading House Creek, which is near the present-day city of Waco. When this trader died some thirty years later, he was one of the wealthiest men in Texas.

Because money was quite scarce during frontier times, deer hides were often used instead of coins to purchase items. Some examples of the 1716 barter rates for trade goods in the Southeast include a price of twenty hides for a pistol or thirty to buy a long gun, plus one more hide to trade for fifty bullets. It took fourteen hides to get a white duffel blanket, four for a shirt, and twelve for a calico petticoat. Two hides would buy a narrow hoe, but a broad hoe cost four. Liquor was also commonly swapped for hides, and four buckskins could be traded for a gallon of rum that had not been watered down. A bottle of rum that was one-third water was worth one hide, and two deer hides would buy one quart of inferior grade brandy.

When an attempt was made to establish the sovereign "State of Franklin" in the Tennessee area in 1784, the new government planned to finance itself with hides. The governor's annual salary was set at a thousand deer hides, and the chief justice was to receive five hundred. Minor state officials were to be paid with beaver, otter, and raccoon skins. Land taxes in the state of Franklin could also be paid in hides, with a deer skin worth six shillings. This same value was placed on good, clean beaver and otter skins.

Like the American Indians, white settlers used deer hides to make articles of clothing—leather stocking caps, gloves, breeches, aprons, suits, waistcoats, coats, belts, shoe uppers, and boot linings, for example. They also used the hides for rugs, wall coverings, upholstery fabric, and as a book binding material. Most leather products that needed a soft and durable hide could be made of buckskin. Thin, scraped hides were occasionally used instead of glass at windows in settlers' cabins, and although they admitted very little light, they were better than having an uncovered opening.

Other whitetail parts were also marketed by the settlers. Chandeliers, umbrella stands, coat and hat racks, gun racks, boot jacks, eating utensil handles, knife handles, buttons, and ornaments were made from the antlers. Deer hair was used to stuff furniture and saddles, and tallow from the deer was used in the making of candles.

As the human population of the new nation expanded, deer were used to meet the increased demand for meat in the East. Market hunting advanced with the construction of railroads, moving into high gear when refrigerator railroad cars came into use in 1867, and the meat being shipped to the East could be kept fresh for at least ten days. Omaha, Chicago, St. Paul, Boston, New York, and Philadelphia were the main markets for venison, and hundreds of tons of it were shipped to these cities each year.

Improvements in gun making made market hunters ever more efficient at harvesting deer. One report claims that more than three thousand deer were killed in five months in an area covering no more than two hundred square miles. The meat hunters were paid two to four cents a pound for this venison, but it was sold at retail markets for ten to twelve cents a pound. Another report shows that 7,400 saddles of deer and 4,750 pounds of venison hams were shipped into St. Paul, Minnesota, in November and December, 1877, where the meat was sold for eight to ten cents a pound. This may not sound like much when compared to today's meat prices, but big profits were being made by everyone involved in the market hunting business.

Why were deer and other game species being exploited in this way? Money was the prime motivator, but many people thought the supply of deer could never be exhausted. Other people believed that all wildlife, including deer, must eventually make way for civilization, so why not benefit before the animals were gone? The future could take care of itself. An editorial comment published in the *Rousseau County Times* (Minnesota) in 1896 said: "Great country this for game in and out of season. We have venison . . . anytime we take the trouble to have it brought in. Nothing like enjoying the good things on the frontier while they last and before civilization makes the game scarce." Another popular belief was that settlement was merely pushing back the American frontier and wildlife was being swept along before it into new habitats. These people could not or would not see that deer and other wildlife species were being overrun by the advance of civilization.

Commercial meat and hide hunters had almost wiped out the white-tailed deer population by the end of the nineteenth century. In 1890, the U.S. Bureau of Biological Survey estimated that there were only three hundred thousand whitetails left in the United States. By 1900, there were no more than five hundred thousand whitetails in all of North America, and it is possible that this number dropped as low as 350,000. Unrestricted hunting since colonial times had taken its toll, and the whitetail was rarely seen. There were less than one hundred deer in New Jersey in 1900, and none at all in Connecticut and Rhode Island.

Although some of the first "hunting laws" concerning whitetails were passed as early as 1646, a look at some of these early regulations shows that they were not designed to protect the deer or increase its numbers. Instead, they were written for the protection of people. For example, fire-hunting was banned because there was a danger of setting pastures and settlement buildings on fire. Pits, snares, and traps were banned because they could create a danger to citizens and livestock. Hunting close to a settled area was banned to protect people from stray bullets. Leaving a skinned deer's carcass in the woods or fields near a settlement was banned because wolves could be attracted to it, and their presence might prove dangerous to the people.

Fortunately, the scarcity of deer in the late 1800s finally sparked an environmental conscience in the nation's citizens. The first state law to set a limit on the number of white-tailed deer that could be harvested during a hunting season was passed by Maine in 1873. In 1881 the Texas Legislature passed a regulation mandating a five-month closed season on deer hunting, and by 1903 Texas had set a bag limit of six bucks per hunter. This bag limit was reduced to three bucks per hunter per season by 1907. Between 1880 and 1920, most states and Canadian provinces hired people to start enforcing their deer hunting laws, but the real turning point in the decline of the deer came in 1900 when the Lacey Act was passed. This federal law regulated interstate commerce in game animals, and the days of market hunting and harvesting deer for commercial gain were over.

By the 1940s, deer numbers had increased enough to allow many people to supplement their limited meat rations with venison during World War II. Some fifty-four million pounds of dressed game meat, much of it deer, were taken from the nation's forests in 1942. Patriotic hunters also donated 238,262 deer hides to the military during the 1943–44 hunting season so that the buckskins could be used to make gloves, jackets, and mukluks for the troops.

It is estimated that there may be twenty to twenty-five million white-tailed deer living throughout the United States today, and many changes are responsible for bringing them from near extermination to their present numbers. Among these changes are land uses that are more suitable for deer, an increased awareness of the deer's needs, hunting closely regulated by seasons and bag limits, and the strict enforcement of game laws.

New Jersey, one of the most heavily urbanized and densely populated states in the Union, has a deer population that has grown from less than 100 deer in 1900 to between 140,000 and 160,000 deer. Effective state wildlife management and a mixed suburban and agricultural habitat have contributed to the increase, but this large population of deer is not without its problems. Although the state has many acres of seminatural land with relatively undisturbed woodlands, much of its deer habitat is patchwork in nature, and a large portion of the choice edge habitat is being developed and suburbanized at a rapid rate. Many deer also live on state and county park lands or other areas where they are protected, and where their population can quickly surpass the limits of their environment.

When too many deer come into contact with too many people, conflicts arise. New York's Fire Island has a population of some six hundred nearly tame deer ravaging the plants and gardens of summer residents. As deer munch their way through the ornamental trees, bushes, flowers, and vegetable gardens of suburbia, whether it is in the North or South, they start to become pests. When dangerous road accidents involving deer increase as commuters drive to and from work, the thrill of seeing a deer leaping across the roadway counts for little. Like weeds, which are merely unwanted plants growing in the wrong places, too many deer living in the wrong places may need to be removed. However, efforts to cull deer are often met with strong opposition.

Solutions to the problems faced by modern game managers are not easy to find because different segments of the human population view the white-tailed deer in completely different ways. To animal rights enthusiasts, deer are creatures that must be preserved at all costs; but farmers who are suffering major crop losses and homeowners watching their expensive landscaping plants being eaten may see the deer as a four-legged nuisance they would prefer to do without. Idealists see deer as wild and beautiful and belonging in the woods where nature will take care of them, but game managers know that nature's solutions when populations exceed the carrying capacity of their habitat are harsh. Hunters can appreciate the wild and majestic nature of the deer, but they also recognize its outdoor recreational value and regard it as a supply of high-quality lean meat for the freezer.

As regards hunting, the white-tailed deer is probably the most popular big game animal in the world, and the benefits from deer hunting are worth billions of dollars to this nation's economy each year. Hunters throughout the United States also contribute to the cost of wildlife management and research studies through the taxes they pay for the purchase of hunting firearms and ammunition. This tax, which was established at the request of hunters, has been in effect since 1937 under the Pittman-Robertson Act, and the preliminary apportionment to all states for wildlife restoration and hunter education programs for fiscal year 1995 totaled $159 million. The money was derived from an 11 percent tax on sporting arms and ammunition, a 10 percent tax on pistols and revolvers, and an 11 percent tax on certain archery equipment.

Deer hunting, in short, is big business, especially in Texas, where records show that in 1991 some 586,000 Texans spent more than five million days hunting, an average of eight and a half days per hunter. The Chamber of Commerce in Llano on the Edwards Plateau receives more than three thousand requests for hunting lease information each year. It is not surprising that Llano calls itself the "Deer Hunting Capital of Texas." The Texas Hill Country town of Fredericksburg, located in Gillespie County, estimates that deer hunting benefits that county to the tune of $9 to $12 million annually. A breakdown of this revenue apportions 39 percent to landowners and 61 percent to local businesses, such as grocery stores, motels, restaurants, sporting goods stores, and gasoline stations. Packaged deer hunts for three to five days cost $3,000 to $4,000, and a hunter will pay $5,000 to hunt on a lease in South Texas where the state's trophy deer are usually found.

There are at least ten million deer hunters in the United States, and a small portion of them are interested in taking only those deer with trophy antlers. These hunters pay high prices to hunt where landowners manage their ranges to produce healthy deer with large racks. The landowners make sure high-quality vegetation is available when the bucks are growing their antlers, and they do not allow the bucks to be hunted until the animals are old enough to produce trophy racks.

Although almost every hunter wants to bag a deer with a large set of antlers to brag about, antlers are not as important to those individuals who are hunting for meat for their home freezer. Eighty percent of the bucks taken during each hunting season in Texas are less than four and a half years old, and about 43 percent of them are yearlings. The average hunter is happy with whatever deer he or she is able to bring down, and accepts the fact that does should be harvested to maintain a healthy deer population ratio.

Most hunters eat the meat from the deer they harvest or they pass it along to someone else who does. Some families prefer venison to beef because of the low fat content of deer meat. When the proud hunters do not have the culinary skills to equal their expertise in securing the venison, the result of their cooking efforts may be tough, dry meat with a "gamy" flavor, or meat that has been drowned in all manner of sauces until it is no longer distinguishable as venison. Anyone unfortunate enough to eat the offerings these cooks have prepared does not come away with an appreciation for the finer qualities of deer meat.

Venison can be a delight to the palate when the deer carcass has been properly cared for in the field, refrigerated and aged for a few days to tenderize and enhance the flavor of the meat, and not overcooked. Those who pride themselves in the preparation of venison claim that overcooking can turn a delicious deer roast in to a hunk of meat that no amount of sauces or cooking wines can make edible. By the same token, leaving tender backstrap steaks on the grill a few minutes too long can turn them as tough as shoe leather. Venison must be cooked slowly until the moment when its deep red color fades to pink, preserving the natural juices and making it more tender than it would be at the overcooked stage. Recipes for preparing venison can be found in many wild game cookbooks, and various cuts can be baked, roasted, barbe-cued, or fried. In southern states, venison is often used in chili and homemade tamales, or ground and mixed with pork to be made into smoked sausage or pan sausage.

Besides the meat, other deer parts are still valued today, but on a different scale than they were in early America. Few people wear buckskin clothing as in years past, but deer hides are still used to make gloves, jackets, and other leather items. Hair from the deer's tail is used in the manufacture of various fishing lures, including by people who enjoy tying their own flies for fly fish-ing. Antlers are still used to make items such as buttons, belts, belt buckles, salt and pepper shakers, knife handles, gun and hat racks, and in furniture.

Nonhunters value deer differently as they choose to use this animal in a nonconsumptive manner. Hunting deer with a cam-era instead of a gun is more appealing to them, and they find pleasure in merely watching deer through a set of binoculars. (Of course, this does not mean to imply that hunters and their families do not also enjoy deer through these same nonconsumptive methods.) As nonhunters buy their binoculars, cameras, and other outdoor equipment to pursue their recreational use of deer, they also make an economic contribution. However, because no mechanism exists for taxing nonconsumptive users the way hunters are taxed, very little, if any, of their money goes to wildlife agencies to be used toward land acquisition, habitat improvement, and research that might benefit the deer they enjoy watching. Hunters will continue to foot this bill until other funding sources are found, and wildlife will continue to reap the benefits.

In the foreseeable future, there is no reason to believe that the white-tailed deer will lose its appeal to hunters and nonhunters. Unlike the more controversial wolves and grizzlies, whitetails can live in close proximity to people while still embodying a sense of wildness to the landscape. No large tracts of protected wilderness must be set aside for them to survive, and they do not prey on livestock. As long as people, in the absence of natural predators, can harvest enough deer to prevent habitat damage, overpopulation, and the die-offs that result from it, there seems to be no reason for the species to face radical threats to its continued presence throughout its range.

Bibliography

ABC's of Nature. Pleasantville, N.Y.: Reader's Digest Association, 1984.

Armstrong, William E., and Donnie E. Harmel. "Exotic Mammals Competing with the Natives." *Texas Parks & Wildlife,* Feb. 1981.

Audubon Society: Encyclopedia of Animal Life. New York: Clarkson N. Potter–Chanticleer Press, 1982.

Bare, Colleen Stanley. *Never Grab a Deer by the Ear.* New York: Cobblehill Books–Dutton, 1993.

Bauer, Erwin A. *Whitetails: Behavior, Ecology and Conservation.* Stillwater, Minn.: Voyageur Press, 1993.

Bojovic, Dusan, and Lowell K. Halls. "Central Europe." Chap. 33 in *White-tailed Deer Ecology and Management,* edited by Lowell K. Halls. Harrisburg, Penn.: Wildlife Management Institute–Stackpole Books, 1984.

Brothers, Al, and Murphy E. Ray, Jr. *Producing Quality Whitetails.* Laredo, Tex.: A Wildlife Services Publication, Fiesta Publishing Company, 1975.

Brown, Bennet A., Jr. "Social Organization in Male Groups of White-tailed Deer." Paper no. 21, International Symposium on the Behavior of Ungulates, University of Calgary, Alberta, Canada, Nov. 1971.

Chaplin, Raybond E. *Deer.* Blandford Mammal Series. Poole, Great Britain: Blandford Press, 1977.

Cook, Robert L. "Learn about Whitetails." *Texas Parks & Wildlife,* Oct. 1975.

Cox, Jim. "Nervous about Ticks." *Texas Parks & Wildlife,* Nov. 1992.

———. "Venison: Handle with Care." *Texas Parks & Wildlife,* Oct. 1992.

Dalrymple, Byron W. *Deer Hunting with Dalrymple.* New York: David McKay Company, 1978.

Gamlin, Linda. *The Deer in the Forest.* Milwaukee, Wis.: Gareth Stevens Publishing, 1988.

Gore, Horace. "Summer Bucks." *Texas Parks & Wildlife,* Aug. 1988.

Halls, Lowell K., ed. *White-tailed Deer Ecology and Management.* Harrisburg, Penn.: Wildlife Management Institute–Stackpole Books, 1984.

Harris, Lynn H. "New Zealand." Chap. 32 in *White-tailed Deer Ecology and Management,* edited by Lowell K. Halls, Harrisburg, Penn.: Wildlife Management Institute–Stackpole Books, 1984.

Harwell, Gary, R. M. Robinson, and Larry L. Weishuhn. "Deadly Combination." *Texas Parks & Wildlife,* Oct. 1974.

Herrera, Joe G. "Whitetails: The State's Most Important Game Animal." *Texas Parks & Wildlife,* June 1983.

Hesselton, William T., and RuthAnn Monson Hesselton. *Wild Mammals of North America: Biology, Management, and Economics— White-tailed Deer.* Baltimore: Johns Hopkins University Press, 1982.

Hiller, Ilo. *Introducing Mammals to Young Naturalists.* College Station: Texas A&M University Press, 1990.

Inglis, Jack M., Bennet A. Brown, Craig A. McMahan, and Ronald E. Hood. *Deer-Brush Relationships on the Rio Grande Plain, Texas,* Caesar Kleberg Research Program in Wildlife Ecology, Texas Agricultural Experiment Station, Texas A&M University System, College Station, 1986.

Kalbacken, Joan. *Whitetailed Deer.* Chicago: Childrens Press, 1992.

McCabe, Richard E., and Thomas R. McCabe. "Of Slings and Arrows: An Historical Retrospection." Chap. 2 in *White-tailed Deer Ecology and Management*, edited by Lowell K. Halls. Harrisburg, Penn.: Wildlife Management Institute–Stackpole Books, 1984.

Michael, Edwin Daryl. "Daily and Seasonal Activity Patterns of White-tailed Deer on the Welder Wildlife Refuge." Ph.D. diss., Texas A&M University, 1966.

Morrill, William I. "Hands Off." *Texas Parks & Wildlife,* June 1987.

Marburger, Rodney G. "Wildlife Diseases Dangerous to Man." *Texas Parks & Wildlife,* May 1969.

Marchinton, R. Larry, and David H. Hirth. "Behavior." Chap. 6 in *White-tailed Deer Ecology and Management*, edited by Lowell K. Halls. Harrisburg, Penn.: Wildlife Management Institute–Stackpole Books, 1984.

Millar, Heather. "Burning Question." *Texas Parks & Wildlife,* Aug. 1994.

Nygren, Kaarlo F. A. "Finland." Chap. 34 in *White-tailed Deer Ecology and Management*, edited by Lowell K. Halls. Harrisburg, Penn.: Wildlife Management Institute–Stackpole Books, 1984.

Parent, Laurence. "Lyme Disease Comes to Texas." *Texas Parks & Wildlife,* Aug. 1989.

Quinn, John R. *Wildlife Survivors: The Flora and Fauna of Tomorrow.* Blue Ridge Summit, Penn.: TAB Books—McGraw-Hill, 1994.

Robinson, Dr. R. M., and R. G. Marburger. "What the Deer Hunter Should Know about Deer Parasites." *Texas Parks & Wildlife,* Nov. 1969.

Sasser, Ray. "Buck Fervor." *Texas Parks & Wildlife,* Oct. 1992.

Stadtfeld, Curtis K. *Whitetail Deer: A Year's Cycle.* New York: Dial, 1975.

Synatzske, David R. "External Parasites of Deer." *Texas Parks & Wildlife,* Oct. 1977.

Taylor, Walter P. *The Deer of North America.* Harrisburg, Penn.: Wildlife Management Institute–Stackpole Company, 1956, second printing, 1961.

Teer, James G. *Rangeland Wildlife.* Forthcoming.

Thomas, Jack Ward. "Velvet-Horn Investigation," pts. 1 and 2. *Texas Parks & Wildlife,* Feb. and Mar. 1964.

———. R. M. Robinson, and R. G. Marburger. *Studies in Hypogo-
nadism in White-tailed Deer of the Central Mineral Region of Texas.*
Technical Series no. 5, Texas Parks and Wildlife Department, 1970.
Winkler, Charles K. "Garden Variety Deer." *Texas Parks & Wildlife,*
July, 1993.
Zoobooks 2: The Deer Family. San Diego, Calif.: Wildlife Education,
1985.

Index

NOTE: Pages with illustrations are indicated by *italics*.

between whitetails and mule
deer, 7
browse, 19, 20. *See also* food:
preferences of
bucking, 79–80

calls and sounds, 41, 56, 61–62, 64
camouflage, x, 31, *33,* 62
caribou, 3, 4, 43, 44
Cervidae, 3
chase, 56–57, 78–80
Chinese water deer, 43
coat, 27, 28–32, *33,* 60–61
coloration, 27, 28–32, *33,* 49,
  60–61
color blindness, 34
communication, 37–39, 41, 54–
  56, 58, 61–62, 64
competition, between bucks, 49,
  54, 66–68, *70,* 70–72, 75–76
competition, for food: between
  deer species, 7, 10–11; with
  domestic animals, 19; with
  humans, 5, 19–21; among
  whitetails, 22, 68, 70–72, 75,
  81–82
copulation, 57–58
courtship, 56–57
coyotes, as predators, 62, 64, 82,
  90
cud, 24, 76
Czechoslovakia whitetail
  transplants, 7

danger signals, 32, 35–36, *40,* 41
deer family members. *See*
  caribou; elk; moose

diet. *See* food, preferences of
digestion, 4, 20, 23–25, *25*
diseases, 89–90
distribution, 3, 4, 5, 6, 12, 94
dogs, as predators, 5, 17, 90
dominance hierarchy: among
  bucks, 49, 54, 67, 74, 75–76;
  on feeding grounds, 68–69,
  82; on wintering yards, 70–72
dominant floater, 74–75
drinking water, 14–17

ear drop, 65, 68
ears, 4, 31, 35, 37
economic importance: to
  American Indians, 94–96; to
  early settlers, 93–94, 97–98; as
  food, 94, 95, 98–99, 100; for
  hides, 96–97; to modern day
  hunters and hunting, 102–104;
  during World War II, 100
elk, 3, 4, 43, 44
endangered species, 5
epizootic hemorrhagic disease,
  89–90
estrus cycle, 56, 58
exotic deer transplants, 10
eyes, 4, *33*–35, 37

fat reserves, 21
fawn: aggressive behavior of, 69;
  bedding site of, 61–62; birth
  of, 53–54, 59–60; coloration
  of, 31, *33;* feeding of, 60–61;
  grooming of, 39, 60–61; home
  range of, 62, *63;* kidnapping
  of, 62–64; mortality of, 22, 59,